PITTS

The Ancestors of
Donna Marie Higgins

Compiled and Edited by
Stanton Darnbrook Colson

PITTS

The Ancestors of
Donna Marie Higgins

Compiled and Edited by
Stanton Darnbrook Colson

ISBN 13: 978-1494914004
ISBN 10: 149491400X

Published by AAS White Heron Press
1623 Soundneck Road, Elizabeth City, NC 27909
White Heron Press and associated logos are trademarks
and/or
registered trademarks of American Artists' Studios

Printed in the U.S.A.

Cover Design by Kim Colson

This Book
Chronicles the
Pitts Family
Ancestors of Donna Marie Higgins

[Additional photographs, documents
and research for this book are on file
with Stanton Darnbrook Colson]

Please feel free to send any corrections,
changes and/or updates to the editor
at the email address provided below.

Stanton Darnbrook Colson
cwaveofobx@yahoo.com

Dedicated to
Margaret Ellen Pitts

The Pitts Family

Margaret Ellen Pitts
Age 22, Albany, New York

The Life and Times of
Margaret [afa Marguerite] Ellen Pitts

PATERNAL ANCESTRY: [PITTS: William Henry, Alvah, William, Joseph, Joseph]

MATERNAL ANCESTRY: [GREEN: Mary Idela L. "Ida", Harte {afa Hartt}, David]

MARGARET ELLEN [called "Girlie" by her mother] was born on April 9, 1893 at Nassau, Rensselaer County, New York. She died at age 70 of acute coronary occlusion [heart attack] at 3:50 pm on June 26, 1963 in the Alexandria Hospital at Alexandria, Virginia and is buried there in the

Margaret Ellen Pitts
age 6 months

Mount Comfort Cemetery. Her father was William Henry Pitts of Nassau, Rensselaer County, New York. Her mother was Mary Idela L. "Ida" Green of Rensselaer County, New York.

Margaret Ellen Pitts and Joseph Francis Higgins

MARGARET ELLEN married Joseph Francis[3] Higgins of Schenectady, Schenectady County, New

3

York on April 18, 1917 at Castleton, Rensselaer County, New York. Helen L.[3] Higgins [Joseph[3]'s sister] and Oscar L. Pitts [Margaret's brother] stood up for them at the wedding. Joseph[3] was born on July 7, 1892 at Scranton, Lackawanna County, Pennsylvania. He died at age 86 on August 22, 1978 in the home of his son, Robert[4], at Fairfax, Fairfax County, Virginia and was buried next to his wife in the Mount Comfort Cemetery at Alexandria, Virginia. His father was John Joseph[2] [John[1] {of Ireland}] Higgins of Scranton, Lackawanna County, Pennsylvania and later of Schenectady, Schenectady County, New York. His mother was Mary Elizabeth[2] "Mame" [Michael[1] {of England}] Charles of Scranton, Lackawanna County, Pennsylvania.

The following are memories from her granddaughter, Donna Marie[5] Higgins:

"My paternal grandmother was the definition of unconditional love. She was of the generation of women who were seen but not heard. She showed her love through all she did for my sisters and myself. For many years I did not know that she and grandfather had lost a baby girl. They raised my dad and his older brother, but I believe we three girls somewhat took the place of the little girl they missed so much.

4

"My grandmother was a stylish, petit, sweet, sweet lady. She fed strays, which is probably where my sisters and I got our love of critters. She managed to cook delicious family meals from scratch in a little Pullman style kitchen with doorways on either end, even with a small sink, fridge and stove, the kitchen barely held one person at a time. I remember, fondly, helping to wash and dry dishes after the many meals she prepared.

"There is a story about how, as a baby, since she didn't have a crib for me when my parents brought me for a visit, she put me in a dresser drawer. People who survived World War I, the Great Depression, and World War II, knew how to be creative and make do with what they had. She took me under her wing as she planted her marigolds and her vegetables in her garden. She taught me how to sew by hand, using buttons from her button box. I have wonderful memories of her and me stringing popcorn and cranberries for the Christmas tree.

"My regrets for my grandmother are that I never asked her about how she grew up, so I know little about her early years. She died young, only age seventy. She was buried on my sixteenth birthday. Other than my tiger cat, she was my first experience of loss. I remember my grandfather and all of us were heartbroken."

The Children of
Margaret Ellen Pitts
and
Joseph Francis[3] Higgins

1. (baby girl)[4] Higgins
born, prematurely, on July 17, 1919 at Washington, D.C. She lived only a few moments, dying the same day on July 17, 1919. She was buried on July 19, 1919 in the Glenwood Cemetery [Site 10, Lot 91, Section G] at Washington, D.C.

2. Joseph William[4] Higgins
born, 8 pounds, 7 ounces, on September 15, 1921 in the Georgetown University Hospital at Washington, D.C. He died on March 9, 1998 at Cypress Gardens, Polk County, Florida and was buried in the Florida National Cemetery at Bushnell, Sumter County, Florida. He married Anna Lorraine[4] Hild on January 10, 1939 at Manassas, Prince William County, Virginia at the home of a Baptist Minister [Editor's Note: they were both underage and the court clerk who okayed their marriage license was a little old man with very thick glasses]. She was born on June 12, 1922 [the youngest of nine siblings] at Washington, D. C. [birth certificate #257,991]. She died, age 71, on July 10, 1993 at Winterhaven, Polk County, Florida and was buried in the Florida National Cemetery at

Bushnell, Sumter County, Florida. Her father was Charles Henry[3] [Daniel Reese[2] {afa Hildt of Jarrettsville, Harford County, Maryland}, Henry[1] {of Darmstadt, Hessen, Germany}, Phillip[1a]] Hild of Harford County, Maryland, who was an inventer, electrical engineer and who attained the highest rank in the Order of Masons. Her mother was Minerva May[3] {also found as Mae} [John George[2] {of York, York County, Pennsylvania — who at age 16 was a drummer boy during the U. S. Civil War}, (Unknown)[1] {Stinemire of Alsaice Lorraine, Germany}] Stinemire [also found as Stinemier and Stinemyer] of Washington, D.C. and later of Davenport, Polk County, Florida.

Joseph[4] and Lorraine[4] met at John Quincy Adams High School at Washington, D.C. where he played the clarinet in the marching band. One day they skipped school and drove to Manassas, Virginia, there they were married. Both parents were upset when they found out and required each to live with their own parents until they graduated high school, after which they moved in together with Joseph[3] and Margaret Higgins at their home on Quincy Street at Washington, D.C.

Lorraine[4] was a skilled singer and used to sing on radio shows and at Walter Reed Hospital during broadcasts for wounded veterans. Joseph[4] acted as her agent, booking events. Her daughter Patty remembers being in her father's arms, watching her mother perform in her beautiful long gowns and long opera gloves. Lorraine[4] sung under the stage name of Anne Warner. She and Joe belonged to a horseback riding group called the "Rough Riders," after Teddy Roosevelt's military command.

Joseph[4] enlisted in the U. S. Army on July 17, 1944 at Fort Myer, Arlington County, Virginia. He was honorably discharged as a private on December 29, 1945 at Fort George Meade, Anne Arundel County, Maryland, receiving the American Theater Ribbon. After leaving the Army, he worked as a machinist at the Torpedo Factory [the Torpedo Factory later became studio and gallery space for working artists] at Alexandria, Virginia. In 1951 he obtained his real estate license, opening up an office in his home in Alexandria. Lorraine ran a dry cleaning service out of the same home. At Christmas time Joe dressed up in a Santa Clause outfit, made by Lorraine[4], and sold Christmas trees in the side yard.

Joseph[4] ran into financial hard times and the family sold their home and moved to New Orleans, Orleans Parish, Louisiana, arriving during Mardi Gras, where he took a job as a salesman for Muntz TV. Within nine months they moved, this time to Dania, Broward County, Florida, where they rented an efficiency motel room. He took a variety of jobs, working as a furniture salesman, a milkman, worked for a juke box company, an airport limousine service, was a taxi driver, a cook, a janitor, a house painter, worked for a vending machine company, delivered newspapers and was a car salesman.

Joseph[4], according to his daughter, Patty[5], stood 6 feet tall, with a head of thick, wavy, medium blond hair and had blue eyes. He had a wonderful sense of humor and could sometimes be quite the clown. He was a gentle and patient man, a loving father and loved animals — the family always had a dog. As he was brought up in a polished, mannerly and loving home, he was always polite and conscious about his appearance. Everyone who met him liked him. He later retired to Dundee, Polk County, Florida.

Joseph[4] and Lorraine[4] had three children: Joan Marie[5], Patricia Ann[5] and John Joseph[5].

3. **Robert Charles[4] Higgins**
born on March 16, 1925 at Washington, D.C. He died on February 19, 1982 at his home at Fairfax, Fairfax County, Virginia. He married Bernadine

Marie Ozmer of St. Mary's, Pottawatomie County, Kansas on July 23, 1945 at Washington, D.C. Bernadine was born on November 4, 1925 at St. Mary's, Pottawatomie County, Kansas. Her father was Windsor Wilkerson "Jack" [Jefferson Gadwell, Robert Clark, Richard {of Brunswick County, Virginia}, William {of Greensville County, Virginia}] Ozmer of Dekalb County, Georgia, and later of St. Mary's, Pottawatomie County, Kansas. Her mother was Anna Emma[2] [Peter Edward[1] {of Watervliet, Flanders, Belgium}, Jacobus-Francies[1a]] DeVader of Morris, Wyandotte County, Kansas. Robert[4] and Bernadine had three daughters: Donna Marie[5], Sharon Ann[5] [a twin] and Karen Ellen[5] [a twin].

Margaret Ellen Pitts & sons
Robert — age 11 ½ months
& Joseph — age 4 ½ years

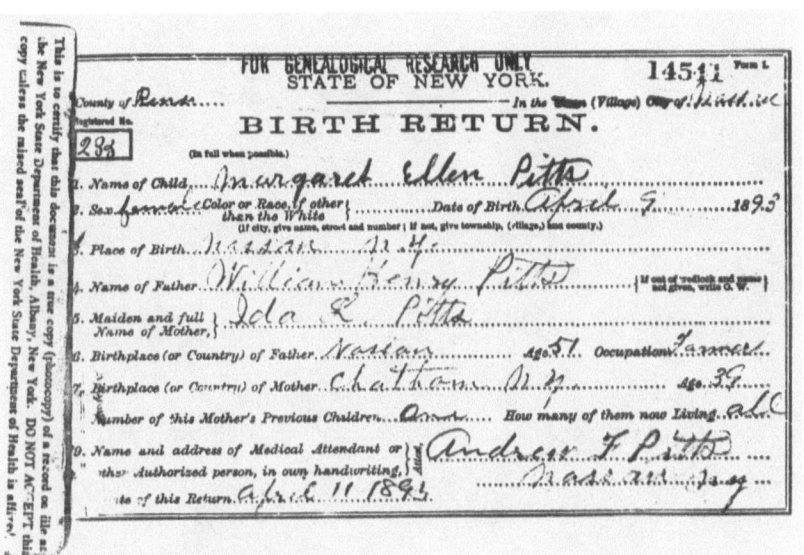

Margaret Ellen Pitts — Birth Certificate

William Henry Pitts (Full Beard)
with Friends & Family

The Life and Times of
William Henry Pitts

PATERNAL ANCESTRY: [PITTS: Alvah, William, Joseph, Joseph]

MATERNAL ANCESTRY: [TRAVER/TRABER: Margaret Ellen[4], Conradt[3], Johannes[2], Sebastian[1] {of Woellstein, Rhinehessen, Hessen, Germany}, Johann Nicholas[1a], Petrus[2a], Niklas[3a]]

WILLIAM HENRY was born on April 22, 1842 at Nassau, Rensselaer County, New York. He died on May 16, 1911 at Nassau, Rensselaer County, New York and was buried there in the Schodack-Nassau Cemetery. His father was Alvah Pitts of Nassau, Rensselaer County, New York. His mother was Margaret Ellen[4] Traver of Schodack and Nassau, Rensselaer County, New York.

WILLIAM HENRY married, first, Ellen Lavina[6] Germond on February 2, 1865 in the Reformed Protestant Dutch Church at Nassau, Rensselaer County, New York. She was born on April 10, 1842, possibly at Flushing, Queens County, New York. She died, age 45 years, 10 months, 14 days, of tuberculosis on February 24, 1888 at Nassau, Rensselaer County, New York and was buried there in the Schodack-Nassau Cemetery. Her father was Willett[5] [Seaman[4] {of Crum Elboon, Dutchess County, New York}, James[3] {Germaine of Hempstead, Long Island, New York}, Isaac[2], Isaac[1] {of La Trembledy, Charente-Maritime, France}, Simon[1a]] Germond of Flushing, Queens County, New York. Her mother was Susan Jane [Abraham {of Flushing, Queens County, New York}] Lowrie [afa Lowerre] of Nassau, Rensselaer County, New York.

WILLIAM HENRY married, second, Mary Idela L. "Ida" Green, widow of Spencer Mickle [whom she had married in 1874], on December 28, 1891 in Massachusetts. Ida was born on December 23, 1854, possibly at Nassau, Rensselaer County, New York. She died on May 22, 1930 at Castleton, Rensselaer County, New York. Funeral services were held at the home of her son, Oscar, at 1:00 pm the following Sunday. Her father was Harte [David] Green of Chatham, Columbia County, New York. Her mother was Sarah Ann [Jonas] Fossmeyer of Nassau, Rensselaer County, New York.

Ida Green

Ida had married, first, Calvin Spencer Mickle in 1874, presumably in New York. He was born on September

16, 1853 in New York. He died at age 24 circa 1877, presumably in New York. His father was Ira [Simeon] Mickle of Kinderhook Columbia County, New York. His mother was Caroline [Martin, Martin, Lucas {Van Salsbergen}, Cornelius {of Albany County, New York}, Henrick Janse, Jan Hendrickse] Van Salisbury of Schodack, Rensselaer County, New York. Ida and Calvin had a child: Claude Spenser.

WILLIAM HENRY was a businessman and owned Pitts Transfer Company at Albany, Albany County, New York. He appeared on the 1880 U. S. Census, he a farmer, age 38, living at Schodack, Rensselaer County, New York, with wife, Ellen[6], and children, Anna M., age 14, Berthia, age 6, John, age 1, and two farm laborers. He also owned a dairy farm near Nassau Lake at Nassau, Rensselaer County, New York. He was a member of the Nassau Reform Church. Because of his heart condition, he sold his farm and moved into a house across from the church.

WILLIAM HENRY appears on the 1900 U.S. Census, age 58, with Ida Pitts, age 45, Marguerite E. Pitts, age 7, Oscar Pitts, age 4, and Harte Green, age 86 [Ida's father], living at Nassau, Rensselaer County, New York.

The Children of
William Henry Pitts
and Ellen Lavina[6] Germond

1. Anna May Pitts
   born circa 1866 at Schodack, Rensselaer County, New York. Her date and place of death is not known. She married Fred[7] Germond [Ellen Lavina's nephew]. The date of their marriage, presumably in Rensselaer County, New York, is not known. Fred[7] was born in 1870, presumably in Rensselaer County, New York. He died in 1960 and was buried in the Woodlawn Cemetery at Schodack, Rensselaer County, New York. His father was Samuel[6] [Willett[5] {of Flushing, Queens County, New York}, Seaman[4] {of Crum Elboon, Dutchess County, New York}, James[3] {Germaine of Hempstead, Long Island, New York}, Isaac[2], Isaac[1] {of La Trembledy, Charente-Maritime, France}, Simon[1a]] Germond of Nassau, Rensselaer County, New York. His mother was Margrath "Maggie" Loweree [afa Lowrie] of New York. Anna May and Fred[7] had at least one child:

   a. Marian[8] Germond
      born in 1906 at Schodack, Rensselaer County, New York. She died in 1924 at Schodack, Rensselaer County, New York and was buried there in the Woodlawn Cemetery.

2. John Alvah "Alvie" Pitts
   born on March 20, 1879 at Schodack, Rensselaer
   County, New York. He died in 1947 at Nassau,
   Rensselaer County, New York and was buried
   there in the Schodack-Nassau Cemetery. He
   married Susan Ann "Susie" Miller on March 14,
   1900 in the Grace Methodist Church at Nassau,
   Rensselaer County, New York. Susan was born in
   1879, presumably at Nassau, Rensselaer County,
   New York. She died on September 19, 1949 at
   Nassau, Rensselaer County, New York and is
   buried there with her husband in the Schodack-
   Nassau Cemetery. At the time of their marriage,
   John was a stage driver. The name of her father
   and mother is not known. John and Susan had four
   children:

   a. Frank G. Pitts
      born on May 10, 1902 in Albany County, New
      York. He died in December 1965 in New York.
      He married Evelyn M. (Unknown) circa
      1925/1930 at Nassau, Rensselaer County, New
      York. She was born circa 1905, probably at
      Nassau, Rensselaer County, New York. Her
      date and place of death is not known. Issue, if
      any, is not known.

b. Stillman M. Pitts
    born on March 10, 1904 in Albany County, New
    York. He died, age 75 years, 3 months, 13 days,
    of heart desease on June 23, 1979 in St. Peter's
    Hospital at Albany, Albany County, New York
    and was buried at Menands, Albany County,
    New York. He married, first, Katherine
    Elizabeth[3] Snyder circa 1924/1930 in Albany
    County, New York. Apparently, they were
    divorced. She was born on July 30, 1905 in
    Albany County, New York. She died on
    February 23, 2000 at Albany, Albany County,
    New York. Her father was Howard Tremaine[2]
    [Francis J.[1] {of Baden, Germany}] Snyder of
    Albany, Albany County, New York. Her mother
    was Catherine[2] [Peter[1] {of Prussia}] Brück of
    New York. Stillman and Katherine[3] had three
    children: S. Donald, Nancy and Patricia.

    Stillman married, second, Frances[2] Cipullo [as
    noted on his burial card]. Their date of
    marriage, presumably in Albany County, New
    York, is not known. She was born on January
    31, 1913 at Randallville, Madison County, New
    York. She died, age 90, on February 1, 2003 at
    Pinellas, Pinellas County, Florida. Her father
    was Joseph[1] Cipullo of Italy and later of
    Norwich, Madison County, New York. Her
    mother was Christina[1] Fontana of Italy and later

of Norwich, Madison County, New York.

c. Charlotte Elizabeth "Lottie" Pitts.
born on August 13, 1906 in Albany County,
New York. She died in November 1986 at East
Kingston, Ulster County, New York. She
married Robert Eugene[6] Teetsel on June 21,
1933 in Rensselaer County, New York. He was
born on March 18, 1904 in Ulster County, New
York. He died in December 1975 at Kingston,
Ulster County, New York. His father was
Erwin[5] [Solomon H.[4] {of Catskill, Greene
County, New York}, Joseph[3] {of Saugerties,
Ulster County, New York}, Jeremiah[2], Johannes[1]
{of Zunderbach, Germany}, John Wilhelm[1a]]
Teetsel of Ulster County, New York. His mother
was Christina [Alexander Kiested, Abraham
{Low}, Abraham Dewitt {Louw}] Lowe of New
York. Issue, if any, is not known.

d. Olive Pitts
born circa 1910/1911 in Albany County, New
York. She died, age 78, in 1988 in Rensselaer
County, New York. She married Edson C.[10]
Currier. The date and place of their marriage is
not known. He was born on June 18, 1909 in
New York. He died in December 1977 in
Rensselaer County, New York and was buried
there in the Nassau-Schodack Cemetery. His

21

father was Benjamin Franklin[9] [Benjamin F.[8] {of Bath, Grafton County, New Hampshire}, Sylvanus[7], Benjamin[6] {of South Hampton, Rockingham County, New Hampshire}, Sargeant[5] {of Salisbury, Essex County, Massachusetts}, Henry[4] {of Amesbury, Essex County, Massachusetts}, Samuel[3], Thomas[2], Richard[1] {of Wiltshire, England}] Currier of Hudson City, Columbia County, New York. His mother was Augusta Laila[8] [Calvin[7], Mathews[6], William[5] {of Granby, Hartford County, Connecticut}, William[4] {of Simsbury, Hartford County, Connecticut}, William[3] {of Windsor, Hartford County, Connecticut}, William[2], George[1] {of Scotland}, Robert[1a]] Hayes of East Nassau, Rensselaer County, New York. Issue is not known.

3. Berthia M. Pitts
   born on September 9, 1881 at Schodack, Rensselaer County, New York. She died on December 22, 1931, presumably at Nassau, Rensselaer County, New York. She married Charles J. Reynolds on September 2, 1894 at Lanesboro, Berkshire County, Massachusetts. He was born on September 4, 1872 at Nassau, Rensselaer County, New York. He died on March 16, 1942, presumably in Rensselaer County, New York. His father was Thomas Reynolds of Nassau, Rensselaer County, New

York. His mother was Jane Ann[5] [Isaac F.[4] {of Kinderhook, Columbia County, New York}, Frederick C.[3] {of Linthigo, Columbia County, New York}, Johann Conrad[2], Conrad[1] {of Lower Palatinate, Germany}] Hamm of Nassau, Rensselaer County, New York. Berthia and Charles had one child:

a. Vera B. Reynolds
   born on March 8, 1908 in Rensselaer County, New York. She died on September 22, 1995 at Spring Valley, San Diego County, California. She married (Unknown) Younie.

4. Wilma Pitts
   date of birth at Schodack, Rensselaer County, New York, is not known. Her date and place of death is not known [Editor's Note: She does not appear on the 1900 U. S. Census and probably died young].

The Children of
William Henry Pitts
and Mary Ideela "Ida" Green

5. **Margaret [afa Marguerite] Ellen Pitts**
born on April 9, 1893 at Nassau, Rensselaer County, New York. She died on June 26, 1963 at Alexandria, Virginia. She married Joseph Francis[3] Higgins of Schenectady, Schenectady County, New York on April 18, 1917 at Castleton, Rensselaer County, New York. Joseph[3] was born on July 7, 1892 at Scranton, Lackawanna County, Pennsylvania. He died, age 86, on August 22, 1978 at Fairfax, Fairfax County, Virginia. His father was John Joseph[2] [John[1] {of Ireland}] Higgins of Scranton, Lackawanna County, Pennsylvania and later of Schenectady, Schenectady County, New York. His mother was Mary Elizabeth[2] "Mame" [Michael[1] {of England}] Charles of Scranton, Lackawanna County, Pennsylvania. Margaret and Joseph[3] had three children: (baby girl)[4], Joseph William[4] and Robert Charles[4].

6. Oscar La Mere Pitts
born on August 26, 1895 at Nassau, Rensselaer County, New York. He died on September 30, 1974 in New York. He married Ada M.[3] Kleinhaus on October 17, 1917 in New York. Ada[3] was born on December 9, 1894 at Schodack, Rensselaer County,

New York. She died in May 1985 at Castleton-on-Hudson, Rensselaer County, New York. Her father was John[2] [Willernud[1] {of Germany}] Kleinhaus of New York. Her mother was Emma J. (Unknown) of New York [her father was also born in New York]. Oscar worked for forty-one years as a telegrapher/dispatcher with the New York Central Railroad. Oscar and Ada[3] had no issue.

Pitts Family at Alva Pitt's (then deceased) farm on August 24, 1930 (Those ID'd: Margie {Pitts} and John Higgins [top right]; Ada {Kleinhaus} and Oscar Pitts [middle right}; (probably) John Alvah Pitts; Robert and Joseph Higgins [bottom front]

Ida Green (Mickle) and William Henry Pitts
Marriage Certificate

26

DEPARTMENT OF PUBLIC SAFETY
BUREAU OF HEALTH

PLACE OF REGISTRY
CITY OF ~~ALBANY~~ *Rensselaer*   CERTIFICATE AND RECORD OF DEATH
COUNTY OF ~~ALBANY~~ *Rensselaer*   Registered No. *23 c*
STATE OF NEW YORK (No.   St.   Ward)   (If death occurred in a hospital or institution, give its NAME instead of street and number.)

Full Name of Deceased *William Henry Pitts*
(If an infant not named give family name.)

PERSONAL AND STATISTICAL PARTICULARS   MEDICAL CERTIFICATE OF DEATH

PLACE OF DEATH *Rensselaer — Died on way to Hospital*	DATE OF DEATH *May* *16* *1915* (Month) (Day) (Year)
HOW LONG RESIDENCY HERE *on road to hospital* [If death occurs away from actual residence, the "special information."]	I HEREBY CERTIFY, That I attended deceased from *May 15* 190_ to *5/16* 190_; that I last saw him alive on *May 16* 190_;
AGE *69* YEARS MONTHS DAYS	and that death occurred, on the date stated above, at *4:30* M. The CAUSE OF DEATH was as follows:
SEX *Male* COLOR *White*	CHIEF CAUSE *Chronic interstitial nephritis*
SINGLE, MARRIED, WIDOWED OR DIVORCED *Married*	
OCCUPATION *Retired*	
BIRTHPLACE STATE OR COUNTRY *Nassau N.Y.*	CONTRIBUTORY *Strangulated Hernia* (DURATION) DAYS
NAME OF FATHER *Alvah Pitts*	*as above* (DURATION) DAYS
BIRTHPLACE OF FATHER STATE OR COUNTRY *Nassau N.Y.*	(Signed) *Geo. Tufts* M.D.
MAIDEN NAME OF MOTHER *Margaret Travel*	*5/16* 190_ (Address) *Rensselaer N.Y.*
BIRTHPLACE OF MOTHER STATE OR COUNTRY *Nassau*	SPECIAL INFORMATION only for Hospitals, Institutions, Transients or Recent Residents.
THE ABOVE STATED PERSONAL PARTICULARS ARE TRUE TO THE BEST OF MY KNOWLEDGE AND BELIEF	Former or Usual Residence Place of Death? days
(Informant) *Alvah Pitts*	Where was disease contracted, if not at place of death?
(Address) *Albany N.Y.*	PLACE OF BURIAL OR REMOVAL *Nassau N.Y.* DATE OF BURIAL *May 19 1915*
	UNDERTAKER *Watkins Bros* ADDRESS *178 So. Pearl*

FOR GENEALOGICAL RESEARCH ONLY

William Henry Pitts — Death Certificate

The Life and Times of
Alvah Pitts

PATERNAL ANCESTRY: [PITTS: William, Joseph, Joseph]

MATERNAL ANCESTRY: [HOAG: Charity Ann[5], William[4], David[3], Jonathan[2], John[1] {of Wales or England}, John[1a]]

ALVAH was born on January 14, 1815 [his death certificate says January 11th] at Nassau, Rensselaer County, New York. He died, age 86 years, 7 months, of pneumonia on August 15, 1901 at Nassau, Rensselaer County, New York and was buried there in the Schodack-Nassau Cemetery. His father was William Pitts of New Britain, Westchester County, New York. His mother was Charity Ann[5] Hoag of Dutchess County, New York. [Editor's Note: Alvah's death certificate shows that his mother was Anna Pitts, Anna being Charity's middle name].

ALVAH married Margaret [afa Margurite] Ellen[4] Traver of Schodack, Rensselaer County, New York on November 13, 1840 in the Nassau Dutch Reformed Church at Nassau, Rensselaer County, New York. Margaret[4] was born on July 31, 1817, presumably at Schodack, Rensselaer County, New York. She died, age 84 years, 1 month, 8 days, of heart failure on

September 8, 1901 at Nassau, Rensselaer County, New York and was buried there with her husband in the Schodack-Nassau Cemetery. Her father was Conradt[3] [Johannes B.[2] {of Rhineback, Duchess County, New York}, Sebastian[1] "Bastiaan" {of Woellstein, Germany}, Johann Nicholas[1a] {a wheelright}, Peter[2a] {of Bambergischen, Woellstein, Germany}, Nicholas[3a]] Traver [afa Traber] of Schodack, Rensselaer County, New York. Her mother was Margaret[5] [Simon[4] {of Kingston — formerly Wildwijk and Esopus — Ulster County, New York}, Jan[3] "John", Jacobus[2], Jacob Jansen[1] {of the Duchy of Brabent, Belgium (or) Noord-brabant, Netherlands}, Johannes Marinessen Adriense[1a] {of Holland, The Netherlands}] Van Etten [afa Van Netten] of Redhook [formerly Rhinebeck], Dutchess County, New York.

ALVAH, age 36, appears on the 1850 U.S. Census for Schodack, Rensselaer County, New York along with his wife, Margaret[4] [age 33], his sons, William [age 8] and George [age 4], and his daughter, Susan [age 6].

ALVAH signed a petition, along with his brothers William and Samuel, and his sisters, Polly, Jane A, Anna, Marilda and Margaret, appointing William as the Administrator for the estate of their deceased brother, Hosea. The petition was filed at the Surrogate's Court office at Troy, Rensselaer County, New York on June 23, 1859 [Petition RENSSELAER 1859].

ALVAH was a farmer by occupation and noted as one of the more successful farmers in Rensselaer County. In 1865 he was originally located on his farm, but in 1883 removed in to the town of Nassau. In Nassau he was the town Assessor for 11 years. He and his wife were members of the Methodist Episcopal Church at Nassau, Rensselaer County, New York.

The Children of
Alvah Pitts
and Margaret Ellen[4] Traver

1. William Henry Pitts
born on April 22, 1842 at Nassau, Rensselaer County, New York. He died on May 16, 1911 at Nassau, Rensselaer County, New York and was buried there in the Schodack-Nassau Cemetery. He married, first, Ellen Lavina[6] Germond on February 2, 1865 in the Nassau Reformed Church at Nassau, Rensselaer County, New York. Ellen[6] was born on April 10, 1842 at Nassau, Rensselaer County, New York. She died at age 48 on February 24, 1888 at Nassau, Rensselaer County, New York and was buried there in the Schodack-Nassau Cemetery. Her father was Willett[5] [Simon[4] {of Crumeblow, Nassau County, New York}, James[3] {of Hempstead, Long Island County, New York}, Isaac[2], Isaac[1] {of La Tremblade, Charente-Maritime, France}, Simon[1a]] Germond of Flushing, Queens

County, New York. Her mother was Susan Jane [Abraham {Lowerre of Nassau, Rensselaer County, New York}] Lowrie of Flushing, Queens County, New York. William and Ellen[6] had three children: Anna, Bertha and John Alvah "Alvie."

William married, second, Mary Ideela [afa Ida L.] Green, widow of Calvin Spencer Mickle, on December 28, 1891 in Massachusetts. Ida was born on December 23, 1854, probably at Nassau, Rensselaer County, New York. She died on May 22, 1930 at Castleton, Rensselaer County, New York. Her father was Harte [David] Green of Chatham, Columbia County, New York. Her mother was Sarah Ann [Jonas] Fossmeyer of Nassau, Rensselaer County, New York. William and Ida had two children: Margaret and Oscar LaMere.

2. Susan Jane "Susie" Pitts
born on March 3, 1844 at Nassau, Rensselaer County, New York. She died in May 1920 at Nassau, Rensselaer County, New York and is buried there in the Schodack-Nassau Cemetery. She married Martin P.[7] Carpenter of New Lebanon, Columbia County, New York on September 29, 1872 at Nassau, Rensselaer County, New York. Martin[7] was born in 1842 in New York. He and his family appeared on the 1880 U. S.

Census, he a farmer, age 37, living at New Lebanon, Columbia County, New York. He died in 1909 at Nassau, Rensselaer County, New York and is buried there in the Schodack-Nassau Cemetery. His father was Anson S.[6] [Calvin[5] {of New Lebanon, Windham County, Connecticut}, Ebenezer[4] {of Coventry, Tolland County, Connecticut}, Ebenezer[3], Benjamin[2] {of Rehoboth, Bristol County, Massachusetts}, William[1] {of England}, William[1a] {of London, Middlesex, England}, William[2a], William[3a] {of Delwine, Herefordshire, England}, John[4a] {of Austerfield, Yorkshire, England}, James[5a], William[6a] {of Homme, Herefordshire, England}, John[7a], John[8a], Richard[9a], John[10a]] Carpenter of Columbia County, New York. His mother was Lucinda[8] [Zaccheus Hanchett[7] {of Sharon, Litchfield, Connecticut}, Daniel[6], Caleb[5], Samuel[4] {of Southold, Suffolk County, New York}, Caleb[3] {Curtice of Salem, Essex County, Massachusetts}, Richard[2], Richard[1] {born circa 1598, probably in England}] Curtis of Columbia County, New York. Susan Jane and Martin[7] had two children:

a. Nellie M.[8] Carpenter
   born in August 1873 in Columbia County, New York. She died circa 1941 at Nassau, Rensselaer County, New York and was buried in the Schodack-Nassau Cemetery at Nassau. She

married Charles[6] Clapper sometime before 1895 [when their only child was born], presumably in Columbia County, New York. He was born circa 1868 in New York. He died, age 28, circa 1896 at Nassau, Rensselaer County, New York. His father was Lester[5] [John[4], Johannes[3] {of Claverack, Columbia County, New York}, Hendrick[2], Johann Hendrick[1] {Klapper of Blessenbach, Limburg-Wellburg, Hessen, Germany}, Johann Wilhelm[1a] {of Eshbach, Calw, Baden-Wütenburg, Germany}, Hans Wilhelm[2a]] Clapper of New York. His mother was Jane Helen Van Alstyne of New York. Nellie[8] and Charles[6] had one child: John L.[7].

Nellie[8] married, second, John H.[6] Clapper [Charles[6] Clapper's cousin], sometime after 1896, probably in Rensselaer County, New York, but possibly in Columbia County, New York, where they were living in 1900. He was born in August 1864 in New York. His date of death, possibly at Kinderhook, Columbia County, New York [where in 1930 he, age 66, was living], is not known. His father was Sylvester[5] [John[4], Johannes[3] {of Claverack, Columbia County, New York}, Hendrick[2], Johann Hendrick[1] {Klapper of Blessenbach, Limburg-Wellburg, Hessen, Germany}, Johann Wilhelm[1a] {of Eshbach, Calw, Baden-Wütenburg, Germany}, Hans Wilhelm[2a]] Clapper of New York. His mother was Catherine J. [Gilbert] McEntyre of New York. There was no issue.

John H.[6] married, first, Mary Kellerhouse in 1887 in Columbia County, New York. She was born in May 1869 in New York. Her date and place of death is not known. Her father was Samuel Kellerhouse of New York. Her mother was Malietia (Unknown) of New York. John[6] and Mary had one child: Clarence S.[7].

b. William A.[8] Carpenter
born on April 22, 1875 in Columbia County, New York. He died, age 28, on April 2, 1904 in Rensselaer County, New York.

3. George Pitts
born on August 20, 1846 at Nassau, Rensselaer County, New York. He died on August 20, 1925 in New York. He married Emma Taylor of Saratoga County, New York on June 11, 1873. Their place of marriage in New York is not known. Emma was born circa 1851 in New York. Her father was George W. [Shubal] Taylor of Halfmoon, Saratoga County, New York. Her mother was Esther (Unknown) of New York. Issue, if any, is not known.

4. Sarah Pitts
   born circa 1847, presumably at Nassau, Rensselaer County, New York. Her date and place of death is not known.

Alvah Pitts — Death Certificate

The Life and Times of
William Pitts

PATERNAL ANCESTRY: [PITTS: Joseph, Joseph]

MATERNAL ANCESTRY: [WINANS: Elizabeth[5], William[4], Conrad[3], Jan[2] {Eynantz}, Jan[1] {of Antwerp, Belgium}]

WILLIAM was born on September 8, 1774 at New Britain, Kings District [which later became Canaan, and later absorbed by the Town of Chatham], Albany [which later became Columbia] County, New York. He died, age 88, on April 1, 1862 at Petersburg, Rensselaer County, New York and is buried there with his second wife, Charity Ann. His father was Joseph Pitts of New Britain [Chatham], Columbia County, New York. His mother was Elizabeth[5] Winans of Green County, New York.

WILLIAM married, first, Salome[7] Wickham in 1789, he age 15, she age 22 [leading one to wonder if she was pregnant when they married], probably in Chatham County, New York. Salome[7] was born on October 13, 1767 in Chatham County, New York. She died in 1813 at Nassau, Rensselaer County, New York and was buried there in the Pitts Cemetery. Her father was David[6] [John[5] III, John[4], Jr, John[3], John[2], Thomas[1] {of Chichester, Sussex County, England}, Thomas[1a],

George^{2a}, John C.^{3a}, Edward^{4a}] Wickham of Dartmouth, Bristol County, Massachusetts and later of Chatham, Columbia County, New York. Her mother was Nancy^7 "Mercy" [Nicholas^6, Nicholas^5, Hugh^4 {Mosher}, Nicholas^3, Hugh^2 {of Newport, Newport County, Rhode Island}, Ezekiel^1 {of Manchester, England}, Stephen^{1a}, Hugh^{2a} {of France}] Mosier of Dartmouth, Bristol County, Massachusetts and later of Chatham County, New York.

WILLIAM married, second, Charity Ann^5 Hoag, the widow of Andrew Couse, sometime after 1810 [when William and Salome$^{6'}$s last child was born], presumably in Dutchess County, New York. Charity Ann^5 was born on August 16, 1777 [her age is shown as 63 on the 1840 U.S. Census] in Dutchess County, New York. She died on February 20, 1849 at Petersburg, Rensselaer County, New York where she is buried with her husband. Her father was William^4 [David^3 {of Newbury, Essex County, Massachusetts}, Jonathan^2, John^1 {of Yorkshire, England}, Richard^{1a}, Law^{2a} {born 1570}] Hoag of Duchess County, New York. Her mother was Hannah^6 [Isaac Tuck^5 {of Rye, Westchester County, New York}, Benjamin^4, Benjamin^3 {of Newport County, Rhode Island}, William^2, James^1 {of Poole, Dorsetshire, England}, Christopher^{1a}, James^{2a} {de Haviland of Guernsey, Channel Islands, England}, James^{3a}, Thomas^{4a}] Haviland of Oblong, Dutchess County, New York.

Charity Ann[5] had married, first, Andrew Couse [sometimes found as Crouse] on October 4, 1797 at Bangall, Dutchess County, New York. He was born on August 16, 1777 in Dutchess County, New York. He died on February 20, 1849 in Dutchess County, New York [Editor's Note: Researchers of this marriage show the same birth and death date for both individuals: whether this is a coincidence or incorrect is not known]. Charity Ann[5] and Andrew had one child: Ann Eliza [also found as Annliza and sometimes even Amelia].

WILLIAM recalled incidents of the American Revolution and often told of his visits, when a boy, to the camp of the soldiers, driving cattle that were to be killed for sustenance.

WILLIAM apparently began to think about becoming a minister at age 15 when he said he was "for some time under heavy conviction . . . my sins appeared great. My guilt of conscience overbalanced all my imaginary happiness" [Editor's Note: Which is interesting, because that's when he was married to his first (and older) wife, Salome[7] Wickham]. Later, at age 21, he again had serious thoughts about the "awful situation I was in," and practiced prayer in secret for about a year. He claimed to have received a revelation that "every person on earth had a right to be baptized and, as well as The Apostles, receive The

Holy Ghost." William determined that he would do his part to assume that the revelation bore fruit — at least in his geographic area.

WILLIAM joined the Free-Will Baptists and in 1814 began to preach while traveling through eastern and central New York State, western Massachusetts, and southwestern Vermont. He became officially ordained on November 3, 1816 at Springfield, Otswego County, New York. He later joined the Reformed Methodists, whose motto was, "We think and let think." He was often persecuted by those persons, as he said, "opposed to the true work of God." William kept records of his travels. The following are excerpts from his journal:

"December 22, 1814. I preached at the Widow Brayton's in Pittstown, Rensselaer County . . . from these words, Acts XXVI.18 'To open their eyes, to turn from darkness to light, from the power of Satan unto God, by faith, is in me.' There was a good number of hearers, and I had great liberty and assistance from God in speaking."

"December 23, 1814. Evening, at a school-house in Hoosack, from Mark I.15. 'Repent, and believe.' We prayed and talked with the school mistress until half past two o'clock. Sister Rawson was blessed and engaged in seeking for sanctification."

"July 20, 1815. At 4 o'clock p.m. at Petersburg, from Thes. II.13 'For this cause also thank we God without ceasing, because we received the word of God . . .' The presence and the power of God were there, and it was a time of shouting . . . ." [Editor's Note: One can imaging the ensuing scene.].

"January 25, 1818. At a place which I think is called Batestown, between Lansingburg and Troy . . . 'Then Philip went down to the city of Samaria and preached Christ into them . . .' Received a contribution of fifty-five cents. 'Woe is me if I preach not the Gospel.' These words kept running in my mind:

> 'If you tarry till your better
> You will never come at all.
> Not the righteous,
> Sinners Jesus came to call.'"

WILLIAM's beliefs were not in accordance with the established religions of the period [Editor's Note: Presumably the Free-Will Baptists were not yet established in the areas that William preached]; therefore, he was not allowed to preach in their churches. Instead, he preached in barns, schools houses, taverns, and even outdoors when necessary. He was a charismatic preacher who brought religious experiences and ecstatic conversions to those who attended his firey sermons.

WILLIAM moved from Greeneville, Greene County, New York to Petersburg, Rensselaer County, New York and spent his last years there with his wife, Litty [Charity], and her relatives. He was known as a humble man. "Pride," he said, was his "nearest and greatest enemy." He left the following instructions in his will:

> "Buy me a coffin and box about 12 dollars, gravestone about 14 dollars, n.b. digging grave, a modest shroud and stockings, to be added to above expense."

WILLIAM and his wife were buried in a small hillside grave in Lewis Hollow in the town of Petersburg. An inscription on his weather-worn stone reads:

> "He will swallow up death in victory"

The Children of
William Pitts
and Salome[7] Wickham

1. David Wickham Pitts
   born December 14, 1789 at Naasau, Rensselaer
   County, New York. He died on January 22, 1858 at
   East Schodack, Dutchess County, New York and
   was buried there in Clark's Chapel Cemetery. He
   married Susannah[7] Boyce on December 27, 1810 in
   the Nassau Reformed Church at Nassau, Dutchess
   County, New York. Susannah[7] was born on De-
   cember 8, 1793 in Dutchess County, New York.
   She died on April 24, 1872 at East Schodack,
   Dutchess County, New York and is buried there
   with her husband in Clark's Chapel Cemetery.
   Her father was Ebenezer[6] [Isaac[5] {of Menden,
   Worcester County, Massachusetts}, Benjamin[4] {of
   Salem, Essex County, Massachusetts}, Benjamin[3],
   Joseph[2], Joseph[1] {of England}] Boyce of Dutchess
   County, New York. Her mother was Sarah[5]
   [David[4] {of Greenwich, Fairfield County, Connec-
   ticut}, David[3], Joseph[2] {of Stamford, Greenwich
   County, Connecticut}, Angel[1] {of England},
   Robert[1a]] Huested of Dutchess County, New York.
   David served in the American Army during the
   War of 1812, and was a prominent member of the
   Methodist church and an ardent Democrat. David
   and Susannah[7] had thirteen children:

a. Socrates Pitts

born on November 21, 1811 in Dutchess County, New York. He died, age 92, on January 25, 1904 in New York. He married Mary Morey. She was born circa 1815, presumably in New York. Her date and place of death is not known. The name of her father and mother is not known [Editor's Note: She may have been an older sister of Mercy E. Morey who married William Finch Pitts, Socrates Pitts' youngest brother]. Issue, if any, is not known.

Socrates married, second, Eliza Sherman [who had first married Andrew Finch]. She was born on August 13, 1820, presumably in New York. Her date and place of death is not known. Her father was Zebulon [Michael Jeremiah {of Dartmouth, Bristol County, Massachusetts}, Michael, William {a cordwainer}] Sherman of Columbia County, New York. Her mother was Mary [Timothy] Phillips of New York. Issue, if any, is not known.

b. Isaac Boyce Pitts

born on October 7, 1814 in Dutchess County, New York. He died on October 7, 1894 in New York. He married Emma[6] Conkling [afa Conkin] circa 1836 in New York. She was born on June 9, 1818 in New York. She died on April 2, 1869 in Rensselaer County, New York. Her father was Nelson[5] [Carpenter[4] {of Rumcot, Dutchess County, New York}, Abraham[3] {of Tarrytown, Westchester County, New York}, Deliverance[2], John[1] {of St. Peter's Parish, Nottingham, Nottinghamshire, England}, John[1a] {of Kings-Wineford, Dudley, Staffordshire, England}] Conkling of Sand Lake, Rensselaer County, New York. Her mother was Laura Bristol of Sand Lake, Rensselaer County, New York. Isaac and Emma had ten children: Annette, Irene, Melinda, Caroline, Susan, Harvey, Juliet, William N., Harriet and Effie M.

c. Marilda Pitts
born on December 4, 1816 in Dutchess County, New York. She died on September 3, 1878 in New York. She married Ezra Ambler on December 27, 1837 in New York. He was born circa 1812. Issue is not known.

d. John Wesley Pitts
born on September 21, 1818 in Dutchess County, New York. He died, age 97, in 1915 in New York. He married Nancy Maria[7] Finch on September 21, 1854 in Rensselaer County, New York. She was born on April 7, 1833 in Rensselaer County, New York. She died in 1925 in Rensselaer County, New York. Her father

was Andrew[6] [Joseph[5] {of Greenwich, Fairfield County, New York}, Jabez[4], Joseph[3], Joseph[2], John[1] {of England}] Finch of Rensselaer County, New York. Her mother was Nancy Beedell of Rensselaer County, New York. Issue, if any, is not known.

e. Lorenzo Dow Pitts

   born on August 20, 1820 in Dutchess County, New York. He died, age 13 months, on September 13, 1821 in Dutchess County, New York.

f. Harriet Pitts

   born on July 25, 1822 in Dutchess County, New York. She died on July 8, 1920 at Nassau, Columbia County, New York and was buried there in the Central Nassau Cemetery. She married Daniel Waterbury [who had a sister Laura born 1803] sometime before 1850 [when their first child was born] in Rensselaer County, New York. He was born in 1809 in New York. He died in 1898 in Rensselaer County, New York. The name of his father and mother is not known. Harriet and Daniel had four children: Eliza J., Caroline, Emeline and Willis.

g. Emily Pitts

   born on August 20, 1824 in Dutchess County, New York. She died on August 29, 1903 in New

York. She married David[7] Hoag. The date of their marriage, sometime after 1949 [when his first wife, Salome Pitts, Emily Pitts younger sister, died] in Dutchess County, New York, is not known. He was born circa 1820 in New York. He died on December 20, 1887 in New York. His father was James[6] [William[5], William[4] {of Durham, Strafford County, New Hampshire}, David[3] {of Newbury, Essex County, Massachusetts}, Jonathan[2], John[1] {of Wales}] Hoag of Fairfield, Fairfield County, Connecticut. His mother was Elizabeth[7] [David[6], David[5], David[4], David[3], John[2], John[1] {of Sudbury, Suffolk, England}, William[1a], John[2a], John[3a]}] Waterbury of Fairfield, Fairfield County, Connecticut. Issue, if any, is not known.

David[7] had married, first, Salome Pitts [Emily's younger sister]. The date of their marriage is not known. She was born on January 10, 1830 in Dutchess County, New York. She died on April 16, 1849 in New York. Her father was David Wickham [William, Joseph, Joseph] Pitts of Chatham County, New York. Her mother was Susannah[6] [Ebenezer[5], Isaac[4] {of Menden, Worcester County, Massachusetts}, Benjamin[3] {of Salem Essex, Massachusetts}, Benjamin[2], Joseph[1] {of England}, Joseph[1a]] Boyce of

Dutchess County, New York. There was no issue.

h. Priscilla Pitts
born on August 4, 1826 in Dutchess County, New York. She died on August 17, 1903 in New York. She married Ransom[5] Devereau on February 10, 1848 in Rensselaer County, New York. He was born on December 23, 1823 at North Nassau, Rensselaer County, New York. He died on September 21, 1908 in Rensselaer County, New York. His father was Hosea[4] [Jonathan[3] {of Goshen, Litchfield County, Connecticut}, Jonathan[2] {of Westerfield, Hartford County, Connecticut}, Jonathan[1] {of England}] Devereau of Rensselaer County, New York. His mother was Margaret "Peggy" [Joshua] Lockwood of Rensselaer County, New York. Priscilla and Ransom[5] had five children: Annette[6], Myron William[6], David Elbert[6], Susan Luella[6] and Emma J.[6].

i. Sylvester Huested Pitts
born on April 4, 1828 in Dutchess County, New York. He died on March 27, 1886 in Colonie, Albany County, New York. He married Mariann "Ann" [afa Mary Ann] Weatherwax on October 12, 1830 in New York. She was born on September 15, 1832 in New York. She died

50

on June 2, 1904 Waterville, Albany County, New York and was buried there in Colonie. The name of her father and mother is not known. Sylvester departed from the family political faith [Democrat] and joined the Republican party when the party was formed. Sylvester and Mariann had six children: Emerson A., Sebastian W., David W., Ida L., Blanchard E. and Albert F.

j. Salome Pitts
    born on January 10, 1830 in Dutchess County, New York. She died on April 16, 1849 in New York. She married David[7] Hoag on January 10, 1830 in Dutchess County, New York. He was born circa 1820 in New York. He died on December 20, 1887 in New York. His father was James[6] [William[5], William[4] {of Durham, Strafford County, New Hampshire}, David[3] {of Newbury, Essex County, Massachusetts}, Jonathan[2], John[1] {of Wales}] Hoag of Fairfield, Fairfield County, Connecticut. His mother was Elizabeth[7] [David[6], David[5], David[4], David[3], John[2], John[1] {of Sudbury, Suffolk, England}, William[1a], John[2a], John[3a]}] Waterbury of Fairfield, Fairfield County, Connecticut. Issue, if any, is not known.

k. Amanda Malvina Pitts
born on September 8, 1831 in Dutchess County, New York. She died on September 10, 1917 in New York. She married Leonard Morey on February 25, 1863 in New York. He was born August 20, 1823, presumably in Rensselaer County, New York. He died on August 6, 1900 in New York. His father was Benjamin Morey of Schodack, Rensselaer County, New York. His mother was Anna Finch of New York. Amanda and Leonard had four children: Edward, Frank C., Luella A. and Mary E.

l. Elizabeth Jane "Betsey" Pitts
born on September 15, 1833 in Dutchess County, New York. She died, age 18, in 1851 in Dutchess County, New York.

m. William Finch Pitts
born on November 21, 1835 in Dutchess County, New York. He died, age 83, in 1918 in New York and was buried in the Clark's Chapel Cemetery at E. Schodack, Rensselaer County, New York. He married Mercy M. Morey. The date of their marriage, presumably in New York, is not known. She was born on June 4, 1843, presumably in New York. She died , age 79, on July 8, 1922, presumably in New York. Her father was Sadra Morey of New York. Her

mother was Phebe Finch of New York. William and Mercy had a child: Charles M.

2. Joseph Pitts

born March 13, 1791 at Nassau, Rensselaer County, New York. His date and place of death is not known. He may have died young.

3. Mercy Pitts

born on December 9, 1792 at Nassau, Rensselaer County, New York. She died, age 52, on September 6, 1844 at E. Schodack, Rensselaer County, New York and was buried there in the Clarke Chapel Cemetery. She married Seth Lewis circa 1812/1813 [based on the date of birth of their first child] in Columbia County, New York. He was born circa 1790, presumably in New York. His date and place of death is not known. The name of his father and mother is not known. Mercy and Seth had seven children: Salome, Cyrus, Lydia A., Elizabeth [who died young], Alvira, Hiram and Elizabeth [Editor's Note: No further information on these children has been found].

4. Susannah Pitts

born on October 30, 1794 at Nassau, Rensselaer County, New York. She died on March 19, 1850 in New York. She married Philip Valentine circa 1814 in Rensselaer County, New York. He was born circa 1790 in Rensselaer County, New York. His date and place of death is not known. His father was Richard [Joel Matthew, Joel Matthew] Valentine of Rensselaer County, New York. His mother was Elizabeth Dailey of Nassau, Rensselaer County, New York. Susannah and Philip had nine children:

a. Jerome Valentine
born circa 1829 in Rensselaer County, New York. He died before 1900 in Wayland, Allegan County, Michigan. He married Lucia Minerva Bostwick on September 22, 1850 at Auburn, Cayuga County, New York. She was born on October 12, 1833 at Mexico, Oswego County, New York. She died sometime after 1910 in Watson, Marquette County, Michigan. Her father was John [David {of Bedford County, New York}] Bostwick of Stillwater, Saratoga County, New York. Her mother was Frances [Moses {of Simsbury, Hartford County, Connecticut}, Moses] Gaines of Barkhamstead, Litchfield County, Connecticut. Issue, if any, is not known.

b. Richard Valentine
born circa 1817 in Rensselaer County, New York. His date and place of death is not known.

c. William Valentine
   born circa 1819 in Rensselaer County, New York. His date and place of death is not known.

d. Betsey Valentine
   born circa 1821 in Rensselaer County, New York. Her date and place of death is not known.

e. Maryette Valentine
   born circa 1823 in Rensselaer County, New York. Her date and place of death is not known.

f. Marget Valentine
   born circa 1825 in Rensselaer County, New York. Her date and place of death is not known.

g. Amanda Valentine
   born circa 1827 in Rensselaer County, New York. Her date and place of death is not known.

h. Lester Valentine
   born circa 1829 in Rensselaer County, New York. His date and place of death is not known.

i. Socrates Valentine
   born circa 1831 in Rensselaer County, New York. His date and place of death is not known.

5. Anna Pitts

born on March 24, 1796 at Nassau, Rensselaer County, New York. She died on March 12, 1883 in New York. She married Daniel Calkins, sometime before 1817 [when their first child was born] in New York. Daniel was born circa 1790/1794. His place of birth and date and place of death is not known. The name of his father and mother is not known. Anna and Daniel had five children:

a. Jane Calkins
born circa 1817 in New York. Her date and place of death is not known.

b. Amanda Calkins
born circa 1819 in New York. Her date and place of death is not known.

c. Charity Calkins
born circa 1821 in New York. Her date and place of death is not known.

d. William Calkins
born circa 1823 in New York. His date and place of death is not known.

e. Eliza Calkins
born on August 3, 1825 in New York. She died in 1916 at Cooksboro, Rensselaer County, New

York. She married Jacob F.[4] Ryan in 1852 in New York. He was born in 1816 in New York. He died on March 30, 1899 in New York. His father was Johannis E.[3] [Edward[2], Michael[1] {of Ireland}] Ryn of Kinderhook, Columbia County, New York. His mother was Sarah Fake of New York. Eliza and Jacob[4] had six children: Anna[5], Emily Emma[5], Charles[5], Jennie[5], Clarence[5] and Alice[5].

6. Mercy Marilda Pitts
   born on January 6, 1798 at Nassau, Rensselaer County, New York. She died on April 3, 1867 at Wilton, Saratoga County, New York. She married Jonas Coon circa 1818 in Columbia County, New York. Jonas was born on December 29, 1798 in Rensselaer County, New York. He died on September 19, 1882 at Malta, Saratoga County, New York, where he was living as a widower with his son, William Henry. His father was Henry [John Henry, Wilhelm Henry, Henry] Coon of New York. His mother was Mary Kinter of New York. Marilda and Jonas had two children:

   a. Mercy Marcia Coon
      born circa 1831 in Columbia County, New York. Her date and place of death is not known. She married Charles N. Corp on April 14, 1870 in New York. He was born on July 29, 1830 in

New York. He died on May 13, 1899 at Ballston Spa, Saratoga County, New York and was buried there in the Ballston Spa Cemetery. His father was Samuel Corp of New York. His mother was Elizabeth (Unknown). Mercy and Charles had three children: Mabel, Mary B. and Henry F.

b. William Henry Coon
born circa 1834 in Columbia County, New York. His date and place of death is not known. He married Antoinette Allen sometime before 1869 [when their first child was born] in New York. She was born on April 6, 1846 in New York. She died on December 8, 1913 in New York. The name of her father and mother is not known. William and Antoinette had a child: George Henry.

7. Hosea Pitts
born on November 3, 1799 at Nassau, Rensselaer County, New York. He died, age 59, on May 21, 1859 in Nassau, Rensselaer County, New York and buried in Clark's Chapel Cemetery at East Schodack, Columbia County, New York. On the 1850 U. S. Census he was living with his brother and wife, William and Charity Pitts. Apparently, he never married.

8. Polly Pitts

   born on August 31,1801 at Nassau, Rensselaer County, New York. She died on June 12, 1861 at East Schodack, Columbia County, New York and is buried there in Clark's Chapel Cemetery. On the 1850 U. S. Census she was living with her brother and wife, William and Charity Pitts. Apparently, she never married.

9. Elizabeth "Betsey" Pitts

   born on July 22, 1803 at Nassau, Rensselaer County New York. She died sometime after 1860. Her place of death is not known. She married Northrup[6] Hoag sometime before 1823 [when their first child was born], presumably in either Dutchess or Chatham County, New York [Editor's Note: It is not clear if Northrup[6] divorced his first wife, Martha Morey, if her date of death is incorrect, or if he married her, second, and their date of marriage is incorrect]. Northrup[6] was born in 1797 in Dutchess County, New York. His date and place of death is not known. His father was David[5] [William[4] [David[3] {of Newbury, Essex County, Massachusetts}, Jonathan[2], John[1] {of Yorkshire, England}, Richard[1a], Law[2a] {born 1570}]] Hoag of Strafford County, New Hampshire. His mother was Polly Wheeler of Dutchess County, New York. Elizabeth and Northrup[6] had at least four children:

a. David[7] Hoag
    born circa 1823 at Chatham, Columbia County,
    New York. His date and place of death not
    known.

b. Erastus[7] Hoag
    born circa 1824 at Chatham, Columbia County,
    New York. His date and place of death not
    known.

c. Loretta[7] Hoag
    born circa 1826 at Chatham, Columbia County,
    New York. Her date and place of death not
    known.

d. Smith[7] Hoag
    born circa 1829 at Chatham, Columbia County,
    New York. His date and place of death not
    known. He married Martha A. (Unknown). He
    and Martha appear on the 1880 U. S. Census at
    Royalton, Niagara County, New York with a
    servant named Eveline Kenyon. Smith[7] and
    Martha had a child: Martha M.[8].

Northrup[5] married, first, Martha[7] Morey circa 1820
in New York. She was born on June 10, 1800 at
Nassau Township, Dutchess County, New York.
She died on April 7, 1840 in Rensselaer County,
New York. Her father was Roger[6] [Stephen[5],

Roger[4] {of Kingstown, Providence County, Rhode Island}, Joseph[3], Benjamin[2], Roger[1] {of Drimpton, Dorsetshire, England}, Thomas[1a] {Mowry}, George[2a] {of Tewksbury, Gloucestershire, England}] Morey of Washington, Dutchess County, New York. Her mother was Mercy[6] [Joesph[5] {of Kingston, Providence County, Rhode Island}, Roger[4] {of Kingstown, Providence County, Rhode Island}, Joseph[3], Benjamin[2], Roger[1] {of Drimpton, Dorsetshire, England}, Thomas[1a] {Mowry}, George[2a] {of Tewksbury, Gloucestershire, England}] Morey of Washington, Dutchess County, New York. Issue, if any, is not known.

10. Margaret Pitts
born on December 27, 1806 at Nassau, Rensselaer County, New York. She died on October 5, 1875 at Fowlerville, Livingston County, Michigan [another record says she died at home in Smith County, Kansas]. She married Stephen[2] Hollis circa 1825 at Nassau, Rensselaer County, New York. Stephen[2] was born on March 5, 1805 in Vermont. He died on January 7, 1875 at Salem Township, Washtenaw County, Michigan. His father was James/Junus[1] Hollis of England. The name of his mother is not known. In 1850 the family was living at Royalton, Niagara County, New York. Margaret and Stephen[2] had twelve children:

a. Albert[3] Hollis

born on February 16, 1826 at Nassau, Rensselaer County, New York. His date and place of death is not known. He was living in Michigan circa 1860/1863 but was back at Dix, Schuyler County, New York by 1870. He married, first, Sarah Jane Obert [the sister of George P. Obert who married Elizabeth Jane[3] Hollis] on October 20, 1853, presumably in New York. She was born circa 1835 at Orange, Steuben County, New York. Her date and place of death is not known. Her father was Peter Obert of New Jersey and later of Orange, Steuben County, New York. Her mother was Maria (Unknown) of New York. Albert[3] and Sarah had five children: Alfaretta E.[4], Orcelia[4], Adalaska[4], Fremont[4] and Obert[4].

Albert[3] married, second, Amanda[9] Allen sometime before 1871 [before their first child was born], presumably in New York [but possibly Michigan]. She was born circa 1847 at Beaver Dam, Orange County, New York. Her date and place of death is not known. Her father was Alfred[8] [John M.[7] {of Cambridge, Washington County, New York}, Laban[6] {of Beekman, Dutchess County, New York}, Elisha[5] {of Dartmouth, Bristol County, Massachusetts}, Philip[4], Ebenezer[3] {of Sandwich, Barnstable County,

Massachusetts}, Ralph[2], George[1] {of Saltford, Somersetshire, England}, John[1a]] Allen of Steuben County, New York. Her mother was Jane [John N.] Davis of Steuben County, New York. Albert[3] and Amanda[9] had two children: Jennie[4] and Adelbert[4] "Delbert."

b. Orvilancy[3] "Orvilla" Hollis
born on February 8, 1828 in Rensselaer County, New York. She died, age 13, in June 1841 in Rensselaer County, New York.

c. Lafayette[3] Hollis
born on January 12, 1829 at Nassau, Rensselaer County, New York. He died, age 76, on January 29, 1907 at Dundee, Monroe County, Michigan. He married, first, Mary Smith circa 1849 at Lockport, Niagara County, New York. She was born circa 1831 in New York. Her date and place of death is not known. The name of her father and mother is not known. Lafayette[3] and Mary had four children: Rosetta Jane[4], Napoleon[4], Herbert E.[4] and George A.[4].

Lafayette[3] married, second, Catherine[6] Brown, sometime before 1865 [when their first child was born], presumably in New York. She was born on March 15, 1846 in New York. She died in December 1895 at Manchester, Washtenaw

County, Michigan and was buried there on December 28th. Her father was Sylvester[5] [David[4] {of Ontario, Canada}, David[3] {of Oblong, Dutchess County, New York}, William[2], Thomas Bachelor[1] {of Cornwall, England}] Brown of Upper Canada. Her mother was Elinor[2] [William[1] {of Ireland}] Stateberry of Bath, Ontario, Canada. Lafayette[3] and Catherine[6] had three children: James[4], Clarence[4] and Lois M.[4].

Lafayette[3], a mechanic, was mustered into the Union Army in Wayne County, New York on September 1, 1862 as a private. He deserted on March 16, 1863.

d. James Alonzo Chatsey[3] Hollis
born on September 18, 1831 in Rensselaer County, New York. He died on December 11, 1911 at Grand Rapids Township, Kent County, Michigan. He married Mary F.[1] Smith on March 21, 1867 at Lockport, Niagara County, New York. She was born on July 12, 1842 in England. She died on March 21, 1931 at Plymouth, Wayne County, Michigan. Her father was William[1a] Smith of England. Her mother was Rebecca[1a] Williams of England. James[3] and Mary[1] had six children: Willis S.[4], Carrie V.[4], Estelle M.[4], Emma Lily[4], Franklin Clarence[4] and

Eva E.[4].

e. Arvila A. L.[3] Hollis
born in September 1832 at Pittstown, Rensselaer County, New York. She died, age 9, in 1841 at Pittstown, Rensselaer County, New York.

f. Elizabeth Jane[3] "Betsy" Hollis
born on September 21, 1834 in Rensselaer County, New York. She died on March 27, 1914 at Pittsfield, Washtenaw County, Michigan. She married George P. Obert [the brother of Sarah Jane Obert who married Albert[3] Hollis], probably circa 1854 at Royalton, Niagara County, New York. He was born circa 1832 at Orange, Steuben County, New York. His date and place of death is not known. His father was Peter Obert of New Jersey and later of Orange, Steuben County, New York. His mother was Maria (Unknown) of New York. Elizabeth[3] and George had a child: Charles F.

g. Lellie Ann[3] "Sarah" Hollis
born on March 24, 1837 at Pittstown, Rensselaer County, New York. She died on May 6, 1905 at Salem, Washtenaw County, Michigan. She married Alfred Hazzard[6] Mott circa 1856/1857 in either Niagara County, New York, or Livingston County, Michigan. He was born on

October 19, 1830 in Vermont. He died on April 29, 1911 at Salem, Washtenaw County, Michigan. His father was James[5], Samuel[4] {of Hempstead, Nassau County, New York}, Joseph[3] {of Cow Neck, Suffolk County, New York}, Joseph[2], Adam[1] {of England}] Mott of Vermont. His mother was Deborah Freeland of Vermont. Sarah[5] and Alfred[6] had two children: Marion F.[7] and Eugene[7].

h. Augustus Pitts[3] Hollis
born on June 20, 1839 at Pittstown, Rensselaer County, New York. He died on April 8, 1881, probably in Wayne County, Michigan. He married Amanda[7] "Manda" Austin circa 1858, probably in Superior County, Michigan. She was born on January 18, 1946 in Michigan. She died on March 10, 1880 at Plymouth, Wayne County, Michigan. Her father was Jonathan[6] [David[5] {of Dighton, Bristol County, Massachusetts}, Jonathan[4], Ebenezer[3], Jonah[2], Jonah[1] {of Tenterden, England}, Jonah[1a], Jarvis[2a] {of Staplehurst, England}, Stephen[3a]] Austin of Cattarougus County, New York. Her mother was Sarah Jacob [Sardis, Major] Davis of Bristol County, Massachusetts. Augustus[3] and Amanda[7] had two children: Jennie W.[4] and Lynn Marvin[4].

Augustus[3] married, second, Henrietta[1] "Nettie" Wolf on September 14, 1880 at Detroit, Wayne County, Michigan. She was born in 1860 at Hamilton, Ontario, Canada. Her date and place of death is not known. The name of her father and mother is not known. Augustus[3] and Henrietta[1] had one child: Augustus[4].

i. Amanda Orcelia[3] Hollis
born on April 9 [another source says April 14th], 1840 in Rensselaer County, New York. She died, age 12, in 1852 in Rensselaer County, New York.

j. Francellia Etta[3] "Fanny" Hollis
born on March 13, 1841 at Pittstown, Rensselaer County, New York. She died on April 8, 1916 at Fowlerville, Livingston County, Michigan. She married, first, George Washington Bayne on November 27, 1863 at Royalton, Niagara County, New York. He was born circa 1839 in Orleans County, New York. He died on November 25, 1864 at Florence, Florence County, South Carolina [Editor's Note: He was a Union Soldier captured on August 25, 1864; there is conflicting evidence that he was part of a prisoner exchange and died at home]. His father was John Baney [afa Bayne] of Dauphin County, Pennsylvania. His mother was

Susannah Benninghoff of Lehigh County, Pennsylvania. There was no issue.

Fanny[3] married, second, Alfred H.[2] Smith circa 1868, probably in Wayne County, Michigan. He was born on May 26, 1841 in Cambridge, England. He died on August 4, 1935 at Fowlerville, Livingston County, Michigan. His father was William A.[1] Smith of England. His mother was Rebecca[1] Williams of England. Fanny[3] and Alfred[2] had three children: Byron Grant[3], Estella Cora[3] and George C.[3].

k. George Colman[3] Hollis
born on October 6, 1842 at Pittstown, Rensselaer County, New York. He died on March 20, 1926 at Danville, Vermilion County, Illinois. He married Alfaretta E.[3] Hollis [apparently, he married his brother Albert[3]'s daughter] in 1866, probably in Washtenaw County, Michigan [Editor's Note: George[3] was a Union soldier in the USCW, mustered out on August 7, 1865]. Alfaretta[3] was born on February 27, 1850 in Rensselaer County, New York. She died on April 29, 1914 in St. Louis [city of], Missouri. Her father was Albert[2] [James/Junus[1] {of England}] Hollis of Nassau, Rensselaer County, New York. Her mother was Sarah Jane Obert of New York. George[3] and Alfaretta[3] had four

children: Arthur L.[4], Nettie E.[4], Fred Gay[4] and George Roy[4].

1. Louisa Jennette[3] "Jennie" Hollis
born on August 9, 1844 [another researcher says August 1st] in Rensselaer County, New York. Her date of death in Wayne County, Michigan is not known. She married William Henry Singer circa 1868, presumably in Rensselaer County, New York. He was born circa 1844/ 1845 in New York. His date of death in Wayne County, Michigan is not known. The name of his father and mother is not known. Louisa[3] and William had two children: Florence and Edith Parepa.

Louisa[3] married, second, as his second wife, Lawrence Wellington[7] Simmons in 1898 in Wayne County, Michigan. He was born on September 26, 1829 at Livonia, Wayne County, Michigan. He died on June 4, 1919 at Northville, Wayne County, Michigan. His father was Joshua[6] [Joshua[5], Joshua[4], Constant[3], John[2] {of Durbury, Plymouth County, Massachusetts}, John[1] {of England}] Simmons of Dighton, Bristol County, Massachusetts. His mother was Hannah Clark[8] [Nathaniel[7] {of Cambridge, Washington County, New York}, George[6], Gideon[5], Matthew[4], William[3], William[2],

William[1] {of Bridport, Dorset, England}, John[1a], William[2a]}] Macomber of Taunton, Bristol County, Massachusetts. There was no issue.

Lawrence[7] had married, first, Frances Ann Rice on December 9, 1853 at Livonia, Wayne County, Michigan. She was born on July 14, 1832 in New York. She died on May 7, 1896 in Wayne County, Michigan. Her father was Clark Rice of New York. Her mother was Sarah Ann Coonley of New York. Lawrence[7] and Francis had three children: Lucy Jane[8], Georgia Botsford[8] and Mary L.[8].

Lawrence[7] married, third, Julia M. Skinner on October 19, 1905 at Northville, Wayne County, Michigan. She was born on June 4, 1859 in Wayne County, Michigan. She died on March 20, 1936 in Wayne County, Michigan. Her father was Ezra Thornton of Wayne County, Michigan. His mother was Rhoda Aldrich of Wayne County, Michigan. There was no issue.

11. Samuel Pitts
born in 1807 at Nassau, Rensselaer County, New York. He died on February 13, 1875 at East Schodack, Columbia County, New York and is buried there in Clark's Chapel Cemetery. He married Jane Marshall circa 1827/1829 at

Chatham, Columbia County, New York. She was born circa 1807/1809 in Columbia County, New York. Her date and place of death is not known. The name of her father and mother is not known. Issue is not known.

12. William Pitts
born on August 9, 1810 at Nassau, Rensselaer County, New York. He died, age 81, on June 10, 1892 at Nassau, Rensselaer County, New York. William married, first, Charity Wood. The date and place of their marriage is not known. Charity was born on July 6, 1816 at Clifton Park, Saratoga County, New York. She died, age 57, on November 24, 1873, presumably at Nassau, Rensselaer County, New York. Her father was Benjamin [Moses] Wood of Clifton Park, Saratoga County, New York. Her mother was Adriet[4] {also found as Arietta} [Cornelius[3], Jonathan[2], Pierre[1] {of Leyden, Holland}, Jacques[1a] {of Wicres, Artois, France}, Chretien Maxmillan[2a], Pierre[3a]] Du Bois of Schodack, Rensselaer County, New York. William and Charity had two children:

a. (son) Pitts
born in 1843 at Nassau, Rensselaer County, New York. He died, age 3, in 1846 at Nassau, Rensselaer County, New York.

b. Mary Averetta Pitts

born on February 6, 1853 at Nassau, Rensselaer County, New York. She died on January 20, 1917 in New York. She married Charles Augustus[8] Boyce. He was born on March 22, 1853 in Rensselaer County, New York. He died in 1890 in New York. His father was Eli Spencer[7] [Isaac Heusted[6] {of Washington, Dutchess County, New York}, Ebenezer[5], Isaac[4] {of Menden, Worcester County, Massachusetts}, Benjamin[3] {of Salem, Essex County, Massachusetts}, Joseph[2], Joseph[1] {of England}] Boyce of Schodack, Rensselaer County, New York. His mother was Fanny [George] Gardner of Nassau County, New York. Issue, if any, is not known.

William married, second, Laura Jane Mead, circa 1832 at Chatham, Columbia County, New York. She was born on May 28, 1839 at Nassau, Rensselaer County, New York. She died on August 1, 1893 at Nassau, Rensselaer County, New York and was buried in the Clarks Chapel Cemetery at East Schodack, Rensselaer County, New York. Her father was George Washington [Enos {of Dutchess County, New York}, Jonathan {of Stephentown, Rensselaer County, New York}, Johnathan {of Greenwich, Fairfield County, Connecticut}] Mead of Nassau, Rensselaer County, New York. Her mother was Marilda [Stephen] Waterbury of

Nassau, Rensselaer County, New York. William and Laura had one child:

c. George Pitts
   born circa 1880 in Rensselaer County, New York. His date and place of death is not known.

The Children of
William Pitts
and Charity[5] Hoag

13. Alvah Pitts

born on January 14, 1815 [his death certificate says January 11th] at Nassau, Rensselaer County, New York. He died on August 5, 1901 at Nassau, Rensselaer County, New York. He married Margaret Ellen[4] Traver on November 13, 1840 at Nassau, Rensselaer County, New York. Margaret[4] was born on July 31, 1817, probably at Schodack, Rensselaer County, New York. She died on September 8, 1901 at Nassau, Rensselaer County, New York. Her father was Conradt[3] [Johannes B.[2] {of Rhineback, Duchess County, New York}, Sebastian[1] "Bastiaan" {of Woellstein, Germany}, Johann Nicholas[1a] {a wheelright}, Peter[2a] {of Bambergischen, Woellstein, Germany}, Nicholas[3a]] Traver [aka Traber] of Schodack, Rensselaer County, New York. Her mother was Margaret[5] [Simon[4] {of Kingston—formerly Wildwijk and Esopus—Ulster County, New York}, Jan[3] "John", Jacobus[2], Jacob Jansen[1] {of the Duchy of Brabent, Belgium (also known as) Noord-brabant, Netherlands}, Johannes Marinessen Adriense[1a] {of Holland, The Netherlands}] Van Etten [afa Van Netten] of Redhook [formerly Rhinebeck] and later of Dutchess County, New York. Alvah and

Margaret Ellen[4] had four children: William H., Susan J., Sarah and George.

14. Jane A. Pitts
born on February 25, 1818, probably at Nassau, Rensselaer County, New York. She died in 1898 in New York. She married Henry Waterbury. They were married sometime befor 1841 [when their first child was born], presumably in Rensselaer County, New York. Henry was born in November 1814 in Rensselaer County, New York. He died in 1908 at Schodack, Rensselaer County, New York. The name of his father and mother is not known. Henry was last found on the 1900 U. S. Census, age 85, living at Schodack, Rensselaer County, New York, widowed and living with his daughter, Nettie J., she age 43. Jane A. and Henry had six children:

a. Charity A. Waterbury
born circa 1841 in Rensselaer County, New York. Her date and place of death is not known.

b. Adaline Waterbury
born circa 1843 in Rensselaer County, New York. Her date and place of death is not known.

c. Marilda Waterbury
born circa 1846 in Rensselaer County, New

York. Her date and place of death is not known.

d. Mary Orvilla Waterbury
    born between 1847 and 1857 in Rensselaer County, New York. Her date and place of death is not known.

f. Samuel Waterbury
    born between 1847 and 1857 in Rensselaer County, New York. His date and place of death is not known.

g. Nettie J. Waterbury
    born circa 1858 in Rensselaer County, New York. Her date and place of death is not known. On the 1880 U. S. Census, she, age 22, was living with her parents and teaching school. Apparently, she never married.

The Life and Times of
Joseph Pitts

PATERNAL ANCESTRY: [PITTS: Joseph]

MATERNAL ANCESTRY: [TOWNSEND: Ann[4],
Jonathan[3], Martin[2], Martin[1] {of Hinton,
Northamptonshire, England}, Walter[1a]]

JOSEPH was born on September 2, 1752 [another
record says February 9, 1751/1752] at Chatham,
Columbia County, New York. He died, age 81, of
cholera on February 12, 1833 at Chatham, Columbia
County, New York and was buried there in the Pitts
Family Burying Ground north of Old Chatham, 20
yards off Pitts Road [Route 66] on property later
owned [1989] by a family named Haverlick. His
father was Joseph Pitts of Massachusetts. His mother
was Ann[4] Townsend of Hebron, Tolland County,
Connecticut.

JOSEPH married Elizabeth[5] Winans circa 1773 in New
York. Elizabeth[5] was born on May 10, 1755 in Greene
County, New York. She died, age 82 years, 9 months,
on February 10, 1838 at Chatham, Columbia County,
New York. Her father was William[4] [Conrad[3] {of
Elizabethtown, Essex County, New Jersey}, Jan[2]
{Winans/Eynantz}, Jan[1] {of Antwerp, Belgium}]
Winans of Greene County, New York. Her mother

was Sarah [John {of New York}] Hawley of Rahway, Union County, New Jersey.

JOSEPH was one of the original settlers of the Riders Mills section of the Kings District of New Britain [a small area which became known as Canaan and was later absorbed by the Town of Chatham], Columbia County, New York. Apparently, he was the first of the Pitts brothers [Joseph, Amasa, and William] to settle in this area. He was the only brother to sign the first title to land on May 15, 1774 in what eventually became the Town of Chatham. He appears on the 1779 Chatham tax list as a land owner in the Kings District [Power of Attorney ALBANY 1774].

JOSEPH appears on the 1790 U.S. Census for Canaan Town, Columbia County, New York along with two males, age 16 and over [William and James], three males under age 16 [Lewis, Levi, and Joseph], and three females: his wife, Elizabeth[5], and daughters, Betsey and Clarinda [Editor's Note: Clarinda was born just prior to the Census].

JOSEPH deeded land on September 27, 1799 to William, his brother, of Coxsackie, and his brother's wife, Elizabeth, 75 acres of land in Greeneville, Greene County, New York. Witnesses to the deed were Lewis and James Pitts, sons of Joseph.

JOSEPH appears with his wife, Elizabeth[5], on the 1800 U.S. Census for Canaan Town, Columbia County, New York, along with two males aged under 10 [John W. and an unidentified male], three females aged under 10 [Waity, Electa, and an unidentified female], and one female, age 10-16 [presumably Clarinda].

JOSEPH was assessed seven days of road work in 1801 [Noted in The Hudson and Mohawk Valleys by Cuylar Reynolds]. He also appeared that year on the Chatham Road Tax List, living at Beat [Road] Number 4 with his brothers, Amasa Pitts and William Pitts.

JOSEPH bought 97 acres in Otsego County, New York on September 8, 1802.

JOSEPH appears with his wife, Elizabeth[5], on the 1810 U.S. Census for Canaan Town, Columbia County, New York along with one male, aged 10-16 [presumably John W.], one female aged 10-16 [unidentified], and one female aged 16-26 [presumably Waity, unmarried].

JOSEPH and Elizabeth[5] Pitts of Chatham, Columbia County, New York, sold to Levi Pitts [his son] of Middlefield, Otsego County, New York, land in Chatham, Columbia County, New York for $2,500.00. The deed was dated on July 12, 1817 [COLUMBIA E1:195 1817].

JOSEPH appears with his wife, Elizabeth[5], on the 1820 U.S. Census for Canaan Town, Columbia County, New York along with two females, aged 16-26 [presumably Waity, unmarried, and another unidentified female].

JOSEPH bought 25 acres in Otsego County, New York on December 4, 1822.

JOSEPH and his family were Reformed Church Baptists and were all actively engaged in church affairs. His will was dated on April 25, 1827 at Chatham, Columbia County, New York and probated on March 20, 1833. In his will he left all his possessions, real and personal, to his wife, Elizabeth[5], for her support and for the support of his daughter, Waity [who never married]. He also spelled out the distribution of his estate after the death of his wife. His daughter, Waity, was to receive one cherry chest and any wearing apparel, and in addition, one good feather bed and bedstead, plenty of furniture and the balance of the estate [Editor's Note: Joseph was being sure that his unmarried daughter was to be taken care of for the rest of her life]. He also names sons, John W., Levi, William, Samuel, and James, and his other daughters, Betsey, Clarinda and Electa.

JOSEPH's tombstone reads, "He was a Baptist member, an honest man, a good husband and father and a believer."

JOSEPH's estate was administered by James B. Van Valkenberg [his son-in-law] who was appointed in Joseph's will as the executor of his estate. In an indenture dated March 25, 1835 the other heirs to Joseph's estate sign, agreeing to sell certain properties in Chatham to Levi Pitts for $1,080.00. In documents dated from September 24, 1835 to October 21, 1835, his sons William Pitts and Levi Pitts sign off, agreeing to the terms of their father's will [Indenture COLUMBIA PG26 1835 and Document COLUMBIA PG233 1835].

The Children of
Joseph Pitts
and Elizabeth[5] Winans

1. **William Pitts**
   born on September 8, 1774 at New Britain, Kings District [which later became Canaan, and later absorbed by the Town of Chatham], Albany [which later became Columbia] County, New York. He died, age 88, on April 1, 1862 at Petersburg, Rensselaer County, New York and is buried there with his second wife, Charity Ann[5]. He married, first, Salome[7] Wickham circa 1787, probably in Chatham County, New York. Salome[7] was born on October 13, 1767 in Chatham County,

New York. She died in 1813 at Nassau, Rensselaer County, New York and was buried there in the Pitts Cemetery. Her father was David[6] [John[5] III, John[4], Jr, John[3], John[2], Thomas[1] {of Chichester, Sussex County, England}, Thomas[1a], George[2a], John C.[3a], Edward[4a]] Wickham of Dartmouth, Bristol County, Massachusetts and later of Chatham, Columbia County, New York. Her mother was Nancy[7] "Mercy" [Nicholas[6], Nicholas[5], Hugh[4] {Mosher}, Nicholas[3], Hugh[2] {of Newport, Newport County, Rhode Island}, Ezekiel[1] {of Manchester, England}, Stephen[1a], Hugh[2a] {of France}] Mosier of Dartmouth, Bristol County, Massachusetts and later of Chatham County, New York. William and Salome[7] had twelve children: David Wickham, Joseph, Mercy, Susannah, Anna, Marilda, Hosea, Polly, Elizabeth "Betsey," Margaret, Samuel and William.

William married, second, Charity Ann[5] "Litty" Hoag, sometime after 1810 in New York. Charity[5] was born on August 16, 1777 in Dutchess County, New York. She died on February 20, 1849 at Petersburg, Rensselaer County, New York. Her father was William[4] [David[3], Jonathan[2], John[1] {of Wales or England}, John[1a]] Hoag of Duchess County, New York. Her mother was Hannah[6] [Isaac Tuck[5], Benjamin[4], Benjamin[3] {of Newport County, Rhode Island}, William[2], James[1] {of Poole,

Dorsetshire, England}, Christopher[1a], James[2a] {de Haviland of Guernsey, Channel Islands, England}, James[3a], Thomas[4a]] Haviland of Oblong, Dutchess County, New York. William and Charity[5] had two children: Alvah and Jane A.

Charity Ann[5] had married, first, Andrew Couse [afa Crouse] on October 4, 1797 at Bangall, Dutchess County, New York. He was born on August 16, 1777 in Dutchess County, New York. He died on February 20, 1849 in Dutchess County, New York [Editor's Note: Researchers of this marriage show the same birth and death date for both individuals: whether this is a coincidence or incorrect is not known]. The name of his father and mother is not known. Charity Ann[5] and Andrew had a child: Ann Eliza.

2. James B. Pitts
   born on December 4, 1776 at New Britain, Kings District Albany [later Columbia] County, New York. He died, age 65, on October 13, 1841 at Middlefield, Otsego County, New York and was buried there in the Middlefield Cemetery. James married Betsey North on May 20, 1798, probably in Columbia County, New York. She was born circa 1782 in New York. She died, age 90, on February 8, 1872 at Middlefield, Otego County, New York. The name of her father and mother is not known.

"Captain" James Pitts removed to Middlefield, Otsego County, New York circa 1802 when the whole countryside was wilderness. James and Betsey had six children:

a. James W. Pitts
   date and place of birth and death is not known.

b. Benjamin Pitts
   born on December 1, 1803 in New York. He died on March 30, 1871 in Otsego County, New York. He married Catherine[1] Shielf sometime before 1827 [when their first child was born] in Otsego County, New York. She was born on December 29, 1807 in Cornwald, England. She died on January 29, 1875 in Otsego County, New York. The name of her father and mother is not known. Benjamin and Catherine[1] had seven children: Mary Ann, Clarinda V., Harriet A., John, Ordelia, Georgiana and Viola.

c. Elizabeth Pitts
   born circa 1813 in New York. She died on July 18, 1868 in Otsego County, New York. She married Barnabas Manning Gilbert sometime before 1848 [when their first child was born] at Middlefield, Otsego County, New York. He was born on May 27, 1810 in New York. He died, age 76, on November 19, 1886 at Middlefield,

Otsego County, New York. His father was Daniel Gilbert of Middlefield, Otsego County, New York. The name of his mother is not known. Elizabeth and Barnabas has a child: Frederick Augustus.

d. Thomas H. Pitts
born in April 1823 in New York. He died in 1907 at Middlefield, Otsego County, New York. He married Ann E. Shipman in 1848 at Middlefield, Otsego County, New York. She was born on August 22, 1828 at Middlefield, Otsego County, New York. She died on March 11, 1921 at Middlefield, Otsego County, New York. Her father was William [Samuel {of Saybrook, Middlesex County, Connecticut}, Samuel, Samuel] Shipman at Middlefield, Otsego County, New York. Her mother was Ruby Clark of New York. Thomas and Ann had at least one child: Burdett Shipman.

e. (daughter) Pitts
date and place of birth and death is not known.

f. (daughter) Pitts
date and place of birth and death is not known.

g. (daughter) Pitts
date and place of birth and death is not known.

3. Lewis Pitts

born on May 24, 1780 at New Britain, Kings District, Albany [later Columbia] County [another researcher says Seneca County], New York. He died, age 86, on April 20, 1866 at Danby, Tompkins County, New York. He married Thankful[7] Wickham circa 1800/ 1801, probably in Chatham County, New York. She was born on July 7, 1780 at Charham, Columbia County, New York. She died in 1852, presumably in New York. Her father was David[6] [John[5] III, John[4], Jr, John[3], John[2], Thomas[1] {of Chichester, Sussex County, England}, Thomas[1a], George[2a], John C.[3a], Edward[4a]] Wickham of Dartmouth, Bristol County, Massachusetts and later of Rayville, Chatham County, New York. Her mother was Nancy[7] "Mercy" [Nicholas[6], Nicholas[5], Hugh[4] {Mosher}, Nicholas[3], Hugh[2] {of Newport, Newport County, Rhode Island}, Ezekiel[1] {of Manchester, England}, Stephen[1a], Hugh[2a] {of France}] Mosier of Dartmouth, Bristol County, Massachusetts and later of Chatham County, New York. Lewis and Thankful[7] had five children:

a. Fanny Whitney Pitts
born on December 29, 1801 at Danby, Tompkins County, New York. She died on August 2, 1887 at East Charleston, Tioga County, Pennsylvania and was buried there in the Whitneyville Cemetery. She married Alonzo Adams Whitney

on May 6, 1821 at Danby, Tompkins County, New York. He was born on May 6, 1801 at Nine Partners, Dutchess County, New York. He died on May 1, 1881 at East Charleston, Tioga County, Pennsylvania and was buried there in the Whitneyville Cemetery. His father was Abram J. Whitney of Newton, Fairfield County, Connecticut. His mother was Phelina Adams of Newton, Fairfield County, Connecticut. Fanny and Alonzo had one child: Nelson A.

b. Levi Pitts
born on June 18, 1807 in New York. He died, age 82, on February 2, 1890 at Binghamton, Broome County, New York. He married Betsy Clock, sometime before 1828 [when their first child was born] in New York. She was born circa 1808 in New York. Her date and place of death is not known. The name of her father and mother is not known. Levi and Betsy had five children; Calphunny, Lewis W., Ladorna, Caroline and Charles W.

c. David Pitts
born circa 1812 in New York. His date and place of death is not known.

d. Wesley Pitts
born in January 1813 in Orange County, New

York. He died on March 13, 1902 at Blossburg, Tioga County, Pennsylvania. He married Ida Mandeville circa 1846/1847 in New York. She was born on February 23, 1812 in New York. She died, age 69, on August 20, 1881 in Tioga County, New York and was buried in the Whitneyville Cemetery at Charlestown Township, Chester County, Pennsylvania. The name of her father and mother is not known. Wesley and Ida had three children: Mary E., Levi W. and David L.

e. Almon D. Pitts
born circa 1817 in New York. His date and place of death is not known. He married Phoebe[8] Compton, sometime before 1845 [when their twins were born], probably in Tompkins County, New York. She was born on March 14, 1830 at Danby, Tompkins County, New York. She died on August 30, 1845 [apparently at or soon after childbirth] at Danby, Tompkins County, New York. Her father was Silas[7] [John[6], David[5] {of Middleton, Middlesex County, New Jersey}, David[4], John[3] {of Gravesend, Long Island, New York}, William[2] {of Ipswich, Essex County, Massachusetts}, John[1] {of Cranneboro, Kent, England}] Compton of Morris County, New Jersey. Her mother was Mary [Amos, Amos] Bacon of New Jersey. Almon and

Phoebe[8] had two children: William L. [a twin] and Fannie [a twin].

Almon married, second, Julia A. Wilcox, sometime before 1850 [when she appears with Almon on the 1850 U.S. Census at Elkland, Tioga County, Pennsylvania]. She was born in February 1824 in New York. She died in 1908 in Tioga County, Pennsylvania. Her father was Joseph [Benjamin] Wilcox of New York. Her mother was Eunice [David {of New London, New London County, Connecticut}, John] Douglass of New York. Almon and Julia had four children: Flora, Mary, Frances and Almon Douglass.

4. Elizabeth "Betsey" Pitts
born on May 29, 1782 at New Britain, Kings District, Albany [later Columbia] County, New York. She died, age 52, in November 1834 at Middlefield, Otsego County, New York and was buried there in the Middlefield Church Cemetery. She married Elias Ismond circa 1810 in New York. Elias was born circa 1777 in New York. He died, age 86, on June 5, 1863 at Middlefield, Otsego County, New York and was buried there in the Middlefield Church Cemetery. The name of his father and mother is not known. Elizabeth and Elias had nine children:

a. Betsy Ismond
   born circa 1811 in Otsego County, New York.
   Her date and place of death is not known.

b. Clarinda Ismond
   born circa 1813 in Otsego County, New York.
   Her date and place of death is not known.

c. James Ismond
   born circa 1815 in Otsego County, New York.
   His date and place of death is not known.

c. Hiram Ismond
   born circa 1817 in Otsego County, New York.
   His date and place of death is not known.

d. Electa Ismond
   born circa 1819 in Otsego County, New York.
   Her date and place of death is not known.

e. Permelia Ismond
   born circa 1821 in Otsego County, New York.
   Her date and place of death is not known.

f. Levi M. Ismond
   born circa 1823 in Otsego County, New York.
   His date and place of death is not known. He
   married Polly (Unknown). She was born in
   circa 1821 in New York. Levi and Polly had a

child: John.

g. Polly Ismond
born circa 1825 in Otsego County, New York.
Her date and place of death is not known.

h. Janet [afa Janette] Ismond
born circa 1827 in Otsego County, New York.
Her date and place of death is not known.

5. Joseph Pitts, Jr.
born on July 13, 1784 at New Britain, Kings District, Albany [later Columbia] County, New York. He died at age 6 on April 13, 1790 at New Britain, Kings District, Albany [later Columbia] County, New York.

6. Levi Pitts
born on May 13, 1786 at New Britain, Kings District, Albany [later Columbia] County, New York. He died, age 84 years, 10 months, 20 days, on April 3, 1871 at Chatham, Columbia County, New York and is buried in the Pitts Family Burying Ground. Levi married, first, Martha[5] Mills circa 1807, presumably at Chatham, Columbia County, New York. Martha[5] was born on January 26, 1790 [as calculated by her age at death] at Chatham, Columbia County, New York. She died, age 31 years, 3 months, 10 days, on May 6, 1821 at

Columbia County, New York and was buried there in the Pitts Family Burying Ground. Her father was Isaac[4] [Daniel[3], Peter[2], Pieter Woeterse[1] {van Der Meulan of the Netherlands}, Wouter[1a]] Mills of Windsor, Hartford County, Connecticut. Her mother was Martha (Unknown). Levi and Martha[5] had four children:

a. Elias Pitts
   born circa 1810 in Columbia County, New York. He died, age 44 years, 6 months, 10 days, on July 20, 1854 in the "City of Washington," Dutchess County, New York. He was buried in the Pitts family burying grounds at Old Chatham, Columbia County, New York.

b. Electa Maryann Pitts
   born circa 1813 in Columbia County, New York. Her date and place of death is not known. She married Loren M.[7] Davis in 1839 in New York. He was born circa 1814 in Hartford, Washington County, New York. His date and place of death is not known. His father was Gardner[6] [Ichabod[5] {of Freetown, Bristol County, Massachusetts}, Ichabod[4], William[3], William[2], William[1] {of England}] Davis of Old Chatham, Columbia County, New York. His mother was Sarah "Sally" Webb of New York. Electa and Loren[7] had three children: Allen B.[8], Sarah M.[8]

and Prudence B.[8].

c. Mary Ann Pitts
born on June 21, 1816 in Columbia County, New York. She died on May 22, 1852 in Chatham, Columbia County, New York and was buried there in the Pitts family burying grounds in Old Chatham. She married Garrett Henry[3] Fosmire in 1840 at Chatham, Columbia County, New York. He was born on February 4, 1811 in New York. He died on August 25, 1882 at Nassau, Rensselaer County, New York. His father was Hendrick[2] "Henry" [Hendrick[1] {Vosmer of the Netherlands}] Fosmire of Kinderhook, Columbia County, New York. His mother was Sarah "Sallie" [Amasa {of Connecticut, who married Rosanna Roberts}, Joseph {who married Anna Townsend of Massachusetts}] Pitts of Chatham, Columbia County, New York. Issue, if any, is not known.

Garrett[3] married, second, Desdamonia [afa Diadema] Eudora Brockway on January 11, 1854 at East Greenbush, Rensselaer County, New York in the Reformed Protestant Dutch Church. She was born on July 22, 1818 at Schodack, Rensselaer County, New York. She died sometime betwen 1880 and 1900 at Nassau, Rensselaer County, New York. Her father was Jesse [Nathanial {of Sharon, Litchfield, Connecticut}, Wolson {of Branford, New Haven County, New Jersey}] Brockway of Dover Plains, Dutchess County, New York. Her mother was Content [Preserved {of Providence, Providence County, Rhode Island}, William {of Swansea, Bristol County, Massachusetts, William] Buffington of Dover Plains, Dutchess County, New York. Garrett[3] and Desdamonia had two children: Charles Henry[4] and Minnie[4].

d. Martha J. Pitts

born in February 1821 in Columbia County, New York. She died, age 7 months, 24 days, on September 25, 1821 in Columbia County, New York and was buried there in the Pitts family burying grounds in Old Chatham.

Levi married, second, Sophia[6] Curtis on August 13, 1821 at Spencertown, Columbia County, New York. Sophia[6] was born on January 6, 1791 [as calculated by her age at death], presumably in New York. She died, age 74 years, 2 months, 24 days, on March 30, 1865 at Chatham, Columbia County, New York and was buried there with her husband in the Pitts Family Burying Ground. Her father was Selden[5] [Deodatus[4] {of Bristol, Bristol County, Rhode Island}, Solomon[3] {of Braintree, Norfolk County, Massachusetts}, Solomon[2] {of

New Meadow Neck, Barrington, Bristol, Rhode Island}, Deodatus[1] {of England and later of Rhode Island}] Curtis of Kent, Litchfield County, Connecticut, Her mother was Elizabeth Wilcox of Rye, Westchester County, New York. Levi and Sophia[6] had two children:

e. Isaac M. Pitts
born in June 15, 1822 in Columbia County, New York. He died, age 81, on June 22, 1903 at Chatham, Columbia County, New York. He married Charlotte T. Hemenway. The date of their marriage in Columbia County, New York is not known. She was born circa 1822 in Rensselaer County, New York. She died, age 70, on February 14, 1892 at Rider's Mills, Columbia County, New York and was buried in the Pitts family burying ground in Old Chatham. Her father was Erastus Hemenway of Rensselaer County, New York. The name of her mother is not known. There was no Issue.

Isaac married, second, Anna Amy Parks[8] Elliot of East Chatham on August 31, 1892 at Chatham, Columbia County, New York. She was born on September 30, 1844 in New York. She died circa 1917, probably in Columbia County, New York. Her father was Samuel Waldo[7] [Benjamin[6] {of Sharon, Litchfield

County, Connecticut}, Samuel Smithson[5] {of Killingworth, Middlesex County, Connecticut}, Aaron[4], Jared[3] {of Guilford County, Connecticut}, Joseph[2] {of Roxbury, Suffolk County, Massachusetts}, John[1] {of Widford, Hertfordshire, England}, Burnett[1a]] Elliot of New York. Her mother was Phebe[6] [Whiting[5] {of Dutchess County, New York}, Whiting[4] {probably of Canterbury, Windham County, Connecticut}, Jonathan[3] {of Concord, Middlesex County, Massachusetts}, "Lt." Richard[2] {of Newton, Middlesex County, Massachusetts}, Richard[1] {Parke of London, England}, Richard[1a], Robert[2a] {of Preston, Suffolk, England}, Robert[3a], William[4a]] Parks of Sand Lake, Rensselaer County, New York. There was no issue.

f. Allen D. Pitts
born in 1825 in Columbia County, New York. He died, age 62, on August 14, 1887 at Rider's Mills, Columbia County, New York and was buried there in the Pitts family burying ground at Old Chatham. He married Hopeful Cummins [afa Cummings], probably before September 1873 [when their first child was born] in Columbia County, New York. She was born in March 1834 in New York. She died, age 83, on May 8, 1917 at Rider's Mills, Columbia County, New York and was buried there in the Pitts

family burying ground at Old Chatham. The name of her father is not known. Her mother was Hopeful (Unknown) of New York. Allen and Hopeful had two children: Sophia and Levi W.

Levi married, third, as her third husband, Ruth[5] Roberts on November 16, 1865 in the Reformed Protestant Dutch Church at Nassau, Rensselaer County, New York. Ruth[5] was born circa 1796 at Chatham, Columbia County, New York. She died, age 87 years, 6 months, 13 days, on September 1, 1883 in New York and was buried in the Nassau-Schodack Cemetery in Rensselaer County, New York. Her father was Philip H.[4] [Philip[3] {of Providence, Providence County, Rhode Island} Peter[2], Peter[1] {of England}] Roberts of Dutchess County, New York. His mother was Phebe [John R. {of Portsmouth, Newport County, Rhode Island}, John, John, John] Moon of Rensselaer County, New York. There was no issue.

Ruth[5] had married, first, (Unknown) Clarke sometime before 1834 [when their child was born] in New York. Ruth[5] and (Unknown) Clarke had one child: Catherine M.

Ruth[5] had married, second, Conrad Allendorph on August 8, 1837 in the Blooming Grove Reformed

Dutch Church at North Greenbush, Rensselaer County, New York. He was born circa 1777 in New York. He died on October 17, 1854 in Rensselaer County, New York and was buried there in the Old Mt. Ida Cemetery at Troy. His father was Heinrich "Anton"Anthony Ahlendorff of Ulster County, New York. His mother was Elisabeth[3] [Johann C.[2], Peter[1] {of near Neuwich, Germany}, Johannes[1a] {of Weidt, Germany}] Becker of the Katsboan Reformed Church at Saugertiss, Ulster County, New York. Ruth[5] and Conrad had one child: Nicholas.

Conrad had married, first, Hanna[3] Fero [afa Anna Feroe] on February 21, 1797 at Rhinebeck, Dutchess County, New York. She was born on October 1, 1779 in Dutchess County, New York. She died on October 3, 1835, presumably in Dutchess County, New York. Her father was Peter[2] [John Christian[1] {of Germany}, Johannes[1a]] Feroe [afa Fuhrer] of Dutchess County, New York. Her mother was Anna Margaret[3] [Nicholas[2], Benedik[1] [of Germany] Stickle [afa Stikkle] of Red Hook, Dutchess County, New York. Conrad and Hanna[3] had ten children: Peter, Elizabeth, Henry A., Catherine, Anna Marie, George C., Jonathan, John, William Hiram and Jacob Rensselaer.

7. Clarinda Pitts

born on May 4, 1790 at New Britain [another source says Malden], Kings District, Albany [later Columbia] County, New York. She died, age 81 years, 1 month and 29 days, on June 20, 1871 [another researcher says July 3rd] at Malden Bridge, Columbia County, New York and was buried there in the Chatham Union Cemetery. She married James Blass[6] Van Valkenburgh in 1807 at Malden Bridge, Columbia County, New York. James[6] was born on August 15, 1787 at Malden Bridge, Columbia County, New York. He died, age 80 years, 8 months, on April 15, 1868 at Malden Bridge, Columbia County, New York. His father was Lambert[5] "Bartholomew" [Jacob[4] {of Kinderhook, Columbia County, New York}, Jochem[3] {of Albany, Albany County, New York}, Jochem Lambertse[2] {of New Amsterdam, New Netherlands, which later became New York City}, Lambert Jochemse[1] {of Valkenburgh, Netherlands}] of Malden Bridge, Columbia County, New York. His mother was Gertrude[5] [Pieter[4] {of West Camp, Ulster County, New York}, Hendrick[3] {Buys of Bergen, Bergen County, New Jersey}, Cornelis Janse[2] {Buys of New Amsterdam/New York}, Jan Cornelissen[1] {of Breille, Amsterdam, Netherlands}, Cornelius Hendrickse[1a], Hendrick Willemse[2a] {Buijs}, Willem Cornelisze[3a], Cornelis Hendricke[4a], Hendrick[5a]] Buis of Rhinebeck, Dutchess County,

New York. Clarinda and James[6] had nine children:

a. Loren[7] Van Valkenburgh
   born on July 30, 1810 at Chatham, Columbia
   County, New York. He died on November 1,
   1894 at Coldwater, Branch County, Michigan.
   He married, first, Angeline[7] Gifford. She was
   born on May 17, 1817 in Columbia [or
   Dutchess] County, New York. She died on
   February 15, 1842 at Malden Bridge, Columbia
   County, New York and was buried there in the
   Chatham Union Cemetery. Her father was
   Isaac[6] [Rowland[5], {of Nantucket, Nantucket
   County, Massachusetts}, John[4], {of Dartmouth,
   Bristol County, Massachusetts}, Benjamin[3],
   Robert[2] {of Sandwich, Barnstable County,
   Massachusetts}, William[1] {of England}] Gifford
   of Oblong, Dutchess County, New York. Her
   mother was Polly Philips of New York. Loren[7]
   and Angeline[7] had two children: Gifford[8] and
   Arabella[8].

   Loren[7] married, second, Annis[7] [afa Annice]
   Husted in 1847 in Columbia County, New York.
   She was born in 1818 at Nassau, Rensselaer
   County, New York. She died, age 35, in May
   1853 at Malden, Columbia County, New York.
   Her father was Sackett[6] [Lewis[5] {of Dutchess
   County, New York}, David[4] {of Greenwich,

100

Fairfield County, Connecticut}, David^3, Joseph^2, Angell^1 {of Somersetshire, England}, Robert A.^{1a}, Laurence^{2a} {of Isle of Wight, England}, John^{3a} {born circa 1519}] Husted of Nassau, Rensselaer County, New York. Her mother was Olive [Simeon] Richmond of New York. Loren^7 and Annis^7 had three children: Ella^8, Evaline^8 and George^8.

Loren^7 married, third, Ann^6 Van Ness in 1869 in Columbia County, New York. She was born in August 1826 at Chatham, Columbia County, New York. She died in 1916 at Coldwater, Branch County, Michigan. As of the 1880 U. S. Census they were living at Coldwater, Branch County, Michigan. Her father was John Isaac^5 [Isaac^4, Jan^3 "John," {of Albany, Albany County, New York}, Jan^2, Hendrick Cornelissee^1 {of Vianen, South Holland, Netherlands}, Cornelius Hendrick^{1a}, Hendrick Gerritse^{2a} {of Nes, Ameland Island, Friesland, North Holland}, Gerrit^{3a} {born 1540, of the Province of South Holland, Netherlands}] Van Ness of Malden Bridge, Columbia County, New York. Her mother was Martha Sherman of Malden Bridge, Columbia County, New York. Loren^7 and Ann^6 had a child: Ella^8.

b. Elizabeth[7] Van Valkenburgh
born on March 25, 1808 at Chatham, Columbia County, New York. She died on January 17, 1885 at Phelps, Ontario County, New York. She married Aaron Cady[7] Gifford in 1824 in Ontario County, New York. He was born on October 4, 1803 in Chatham, Columbia County, New York. He died on September 30, 1874 at Phelps, Ontario County, New York. His father was Jesse[6] [Rowland[5], {of Nantucket, Nantucket County, Massachusetts}, John[4], {of Dartmouth, Bristol County, Massachusetts}, Benjamin[3], Robert[2] {of Sandwich, Barnstable County, Massachusetts}, William[1] {of England}] Gifford of Chatham, Columibia County, New York. His mother was Irene Cady of Chatham, Columbia County, New York. Elizabeth[7] and Aaron[7] had seven children: Louisa[8], James[8], Jesse H.[8], Aaron Cady[8], Jr., Clara V.[8], Charles[8] and Robert Wahu[8].

c. Harrison[7] Van Valkenburgh
born on March 18, 1813 at Chatham, Columbia County, New York. He died of camp distemper [blood dysentery] on September 22, 1817 at Chatham, Columbia County, New York.

d. Minor[7] Van Valkenburgh
born on February 8, 1816 at Chatham, Columbia

County, New York. The child died of camp distemper [blood dysentery] on September 22, 1817 at Chatham, Columbia County, New York.

e. Angeline[7] Van Valkenburgh
born on September 6, 1818 at Chatham, Columbia County, New York. She died after inhaling steam from a tea pot on March 6, 1820 at Chatham, Columbia County, New York.

f. George W.[7] Van Valkenburgh
born on February 2, 1821 at Malden Bridge, Columbia County, New York. His date and place of death is not known. He married Sarah Ann Burgess of Chatham County, New York. Her father was Volney Burgess of Chatham, Columbia County, New York. Her mother was Polly Lester of Chatham, Columbia County, New York. George[7] and Sarah had five children: John R.[8], George Volney[8], Clarinda[8] "Clara," Helen[8] and Harriet[8] [Editor's Note: Another researcher lists a Louise[8], which may be a middle name of either Helen[8] or Harriet[8]].

g. Eli[7] Van Valkenburgh
born on February 20, 1824 at Chatham, Columbia County, New York. He died on January 10, 1902 in Hillsdale County, Michigan. He married Jane Augusta Blackmar on

February 8, 1858 at Newark, Wayne County, New York. She was born on July 5, 1833 at Newark, Wayne County, New York. She died on June 6, 1880 in Hillsdale County, Michigan. Her father was Esbon Blackmar of Freehold County, New York. Her mother was Arabella [afa Abijah] Reed of Green County, New York. Eli[7] and Jane had seven children: Arabella[8], Esbon B.[8], Agnes Elizabeth[8], Harriett Reed[8], Mary Mumford[8], Edith Pitts[8] and Maude[8].

h. John W.[7] Van Valkenburgh
born on June 23, 1826 at Chatham, Columbia County, New York. He died in 1904, presumably at Albany, Albany County, New York. He married, first, Mary Rice in 1845 in Kings County, New York. She was born in 1826 in New York. Her date and place of death is not known. John[7] and Mary had one child: Anna Louisa[8] [Editor's Note: As an adult, Anna[8] died during the birth of a child who John W.[7] adopted and had the child's name changed to Dewitt C.[8] Van Valkenburg].

John W.[7] married, second, Louise Allen Smith of Ogdensburg, St. Lawrence County, New York on March 4, 1884 at Albany, Albany County, New York. She was born in 1826 in New York. She died on January 31, 1913 in Albany County,

New York. Her father was Simon Smith of New York. Her mother was Rachel Knapp of New York. John[7] and Louise resided at Albany, Albany County, New York. There was no issue.

Louise had married, first, Rufus Palmer. The date and place of their marriage is not known. He was born in 1833 at Austerlitz, Columbia County, New York. He died on September 11, 1864 in Columbia County, New York. Issue, if any, is not known.

i. Catherine[7] Van Valkenburgh
born on March 7, 1830 at Chatham, Columbia County, New York. She died of croop on May 28, 1831 at Chatham, Columbia County, New York.

8. Waity Pitts
born on May 3, 1792 at New Britain, Kings District, Albany [later Columbia] County, New York. She died, age 61, on January 29, 1853 at Chatham, Columbia County, New York and was buried there in the Pitts Family Burying Ground. She never married.

9. John W. Pitts
born on June 23, 1795 at New Britain, Kings District [aka Caanan], Albany [later Columbia]

County, New York. He died on March 9, 1875 at Malden Bridge [near Old Chatham], Columbia County, New York and is buried there on his farm in a family cemetery. He married, first, Polly L.[7] Gifford on May 30, 1817, presumably at Chatham, Columbia County, New York. Polly[7] was born on May 2, 1797 at Chatham, Columbia County, New York. She died, age 50, on March 30, 1847 at Malden Bridge, Columbia County, New York and is buried with her husband on the family farm. Her father was Jesse[6] [Rowland[5] {of Nantucket, Nantucket Island, Massachusetts}, John[4] {of Dartmouth, Bristol County, Massachusetts}, Benjamin[3], Robert[2] {of Sandwich, Barnstable County, Cape Cod, Massachusetts}, William[1] {of Milton, Damerel, Devonshire, England and later of St. Helens, Bishopgate, London, England}, Philip[1a] {of London, Middlesex, England}] Gifford of Chatham, New York. Her mother was Irene[7] [Aaron[6], Aaron[5], Aaron[4], James[3], Nicholas[2], David[1] {of England}] Cady of Chatham, New York. John and Polly[7] had seven children:

a. Irene Gifford Pitts
    born on July 11, 1818 at Chatham, Columbia County, New York. She died on August 10, 1879 at Newark, Wayne County, New York. She married Clark Phillips on September 30, 1840 at Chatham, Columbia County, New York. He

was born on August 5, 1817 at Schodack, Rensselaer County, New York. He died sometime after 1877 in Wayne County, New York. His father was John Phillips of Rensselaer County, New York. His mother was Esther (Unknown) of New York. Irene and Clark had at least two children: Mary E. and Emily L.

Clark married, second, Lizzie M. Sanford, on May 3, 1882 at North Adams, Berkshire County, Massachusetts. She was born circa 1844 at North Adams, Berkshire County, Massachusetts. She died on March 10, 1907, possibly in Wayne County, New York. Her father was Isaac Sanford of North Adams, Berkshire County, Massachusetts. Her mother was Emeline (Unknown) of Massachusetts. There was no issue.

b. William Anson Pitts
    born on June 5, 1820 at Chatham, Columbia County, New York. He died, age 20 years, 11 months, 22 days, on May 28, 1841 at Chatham, Columbia County, New York and was buried there in the Pitts family burying grounds in Old Chatham.

c. Jesse Gifford Pitts
    born on June 7, 1823 at Chatham, Columbia

County, New York. He died sometime after June 1900 at Acadia Township, Wayne County, New York [where he, age 77, was residing at that time]. In 1880 he and his family were living at Newark, Wayne County, New York, he a boot and shoe merchant. He married Helen Rosalie[8] Day on June 2, 1859 at Westfield, Hampton County, Massachusetts. She was born on June 2, 1834 at Westfield, Hampton County, Massachusetts. Her date of death, probably in Wayne County, New York, is not known. Her father was David Noble[7] [Martin[6] {of West Springfield, Hampton County, Massachusetts}, Gideon[5], Josiah[4], Samuel[3], Thomas[2] {of Hartford, Hartford County, Connecticut}, Samuel[1] {of Ipswich, Suffolk, England}] Day of Westfield, Hampton County, Massachusetts. Her mother was Eliza L. [Raphael] Johnson of Bristol, Hartford County, Connecticut. Jesse and Helen[8] had a child: Louise W.

d. Elizabeth Gertrude Pitts
born on July 6, 1827 at Chatham, Columbia County, New York. She died, age 50, on June 30, 1878 at Lyons, Wayne County, New York. She married Herman Jacob[6] Leach on August 12, 1852 at Lyons, Wayne County, New York. He was born on November 11, 1817 at Lyons, Wayne County, New York. He died on March

1, 1898 at Lyons, Wayne County, New York. His father was Jacob[5] [Richard[4], Richard[3] {of Wenham, Essex County, Massachusetts}, John[2] {of Salem, Essex County, Massachusetts}, John[1] {of Gravesend, Kent County, England}, John[1a]] Leach of Torrington, Litchfield County, Connecticut and later of Lyons, Wayne County, New York. His mother was Sarah[5] [Benjamin[4], Dan(iel)[3] {of New Haven, New Haven County, Connecticut}, Samuel[2], Isaac[1] {of Bingley, West Riding, Yorkshire, England}]] Bradley of Torrington, Litchfield County, Connecticut and later of Lyons, Wayne County, New York. Elizabeth and Herman[6] had three children: Charles Herman[7], Jesse Clark[7] and Helen Irene[7].

e. John Leland Pitts
born October 11, 1834 at Chatham, Columbia County, New York. He died, age 12 years, 8½ months, on July 26, 1847 at Chatham, Columbia County, New York and was buried there in the Pitts family burying grounds at old Chatham.

f. Emma Jane Pitts
born on April 13, 1838 at Chatham, Columbia County, New York. She died, 3 years, 10 months, on January 23, 1842 at Chatham, Columbia County, New York and was buried there in the Pitts family burying grounds at old

Chatham.

John married, second, Lucy Gilbert on September 20, 1847 at Chatham, Columbia County, New York. Lucy was born circa 1797 in New York. Her date and place of death is not known. The name of her father and mother is not known. John and Lucy had a child: (name not known).

g. Florence Pitts
born on May 1, 1850 at Chatham, Columbia County, New York. She died, age 16 months, on September 26, 1851 at Chatham, Columbia County, New York.

10. Electra [afa Electa] Pitts
born on December 22, 1800 at New Britain, Kings District, Albany [later Columbia] County, New York. She died in 1883 at Chatham, Columbia County, New York and was buried there with her husband in the Chatham Union Cemetery. She married Howland⁶ Ferguson circa 1818, presumably at Chatham, Columbia County, New York. Howland⁶ was born on August 30, 1796, presumably in Columbia County, New York. He died, age 80, on April 27, 1877 at Chatham, Columbia County, New York and is buried there with his wife in the Chatham Union Cemetery. His father was Israel⁵ [Jeremiah⁴, Richard³, Thomas²,

John[1] {born 1630} Ferguson of Cold Spring, Phillipstown, Putnam County, New York. His mother was Esther [John] Filkins of New York. Electa and Howland[6] had six children:

a. Sylvester[7] Ferguson
   born on July 15, 1823 at Chatham, Columbia County, New York. His date of death is not known. He was buried in the Chatham Union Cemetery at Chatham, Columbia County, New York. He married Lydia M. (Unknown) sometime before 1850 [when their child, Mary[8], was born]. Apparently, they were later divorced. She was born in 1829 in New York She died in 1913 in Columbia County, New York and was buried there in the Chatham Union Cemetery at Old Chatham. In July 1864, Sylvester[7] of Malden Bridge, Columbia County, New York enlisted in the Union Navy as a landsman, assigned to the Naval ship *Dameriscota*. Sylvester[7] was listed on the 1880 U. S. Census as single, age 57, no occupation, living with his mother and his sister, Ann Elizabeth[7]]. Sylvester[7] and Lydia had a child: Mary[8].

b. Clarinda[7] Ferguson
   date and place of birth and death, probably Malden Bridge, Columbia County, New York, is not known. Apparently, she died young.

c. Mary[7] Ferguson
date and place of birth and death, probably Malden Bridge, Columbia County, New York, is not known. Apparently, she died young.

d. Clark[7] Ferguson
date and place of birth and death, probably Malden Bridge, Columbia County, New York, is not known. Apparently, he died young.

e. George Howland[7] Ferguson
born on May 2, 1831 at Malden Bridge, Columbia County, New York. He died in 1915 at Malden Bridge, Columbia County, New York and was buried in the Chatham Union Cemetery at Old Chatham. He married Phebe Phillips sometime before 1861 at Chatham, Columbia County, New York. She was born circa 1834 in New York. She died in 1923 at Malden Bridge, Columbia County, New York and was buried in the Chatham Union Cemetery at Old Chatham. The name of her father and mother is not known. On July 26, 1859, George[7] and his brother Sylvester[7], received a patent [#24861] for a machine for feeding paper into printing presses. George[7] and Phebe had two children: Mary Jane[8] and George Earl[8].

f. Ann Elizabeth[7] Ferguson
born circa 1834 at Malden Bridge, Columbia County, New York. Her date of death is not known. She was buried in the Chatham Union Cemetery. Apparently, she never married.

The Life and Times of
Joseph Pitts

PATERNAL ANCESTRY: [PITTS: (Unknown)]

MATERNAL ANCESTRY: [(UNKNOWN)]

JOSEPH was born circa 1723/1725 in Massachusetts [although other records show New London County, Connecticut]. His date and place of death is not known [but possibly Columbia County, New York]. The name of his father is not known. The name of his mother is not known

[EDITOR'S NOTE: In 1648 there was a Joseph Pitts residing in Deerfield, Franklin County, Massachusetts who was a soldier during the Indian Wars who may have been his father. On the other hand, his parents may have been William Pitts of Boston, Suffolk County, Massachusetts and Deborah Skinner of Marblehead, Essex County, Massachusetts; another researcher believes James Pitts of Massachusetts and Maria (Unknown) — research continues].

JOSEPH married Ann[4] Townsend on November 10, 1748 [another record says October 27, 1748, which may have been the date their intentions were published] at Colchester, New London County, Connecticut at the Second Congregation Church of

Colchester as recorded on the books of the First Church of Colchester by the Reverend Ephraim Little, Pastor. Ann[4] was born in 1737 [another record says 1728 in Massachusetts] at Hebron, Tolland County, Connecticut. Her date of death, presumably at Chatham, Columbia County, New York, is not known. Her father was Jonathan Nathan[3] [Martin[2] {of Watertown, Suffolk County, Massachusetts}, Martin[1] {of Northamptonshire, England}, Walter[1a] {born 1570 of Hinton in the Hedges, Northamptonshire, England}] Townsend of Watertown, Suffolk County, Massachusetts. Her mother was Mary[3] [Job[2], John[1] {of England}, John[1a] {of Glastonbury, Somersetshire, England}, Richard[2a]] Otis of Scituate, Plymouth County, Massachusetts.

JOSEPH and Ann[4] apparently removed from Colchester, New London County, Connecticut to Chatham, Columbia County, New York between 1749 [when Sarah was born] and 1752 [when Joseph was born].

The Children of
Joseph Pitts
and Ann[4] Townsend

1. Sarah Pitts
   born in 1749 [another record says 1747, which is before her parent's marriage date] at Colchester, New London County, Connecticut. Her date and place of death is not known. She married Archibald Walker circa 1779 in New York. He was born in 1744 [another record says 1754], probably at Canaan, Columbia County, New York. His date and place of death is not known. His father was James Walker of Canaan, Columbia County, New York. The name of his mother is not known. In 1790, Sarah and Archibald were living at Canaan, Columbia County, New York. Sarah and Archibald had six children:

   a. Abraham Walker
      date and place of birth and death is not known. In 1790 he was living at Kinderhook, Columbia County, New York.

   b. James Walker
      date and place of birth and death is not known. In 1790 he was living at Kinderhook, Columbia County, New York.

c. Mary Walker

born circa 1766, probably in Columbia County, New York. She died on June 2, 1822 at Chatham, Columbia County, New York and was buried there in the Chatham Union Cemetery. She married Simeon[5] Richmond circa 1790 in Columbia County, New York. He was born on February 28, 1758 at Middleboro, Plymouth County, Massachusetts, He died on June 2, 1824 at Chatham, Columbia County, New York. His father was George[4] [Josiah[3] {of Taunton, Bristol County, Massachusetts}, Edward[2], John[1] {of Ashton, Keynes, Wiltshire, England}, John[1a]] Richmond of Middleboro, Plymouth County, Massachusetts. His mother was Hannah[4] [Peter[3] {of Salem, Essex County, Massachusetts}, Stephen[2], Thomas[1] {of North Curry, Somersetshire, England}, Richard[1a] {of London, England}, Thomas[2a] {of Weden, Northamptonshire, England}, John[2a], John[3a] {born circa 1510}] Caswell of Taunton, Bristol County, Massachusetts. Mary and Simeon[5] had eight children: Hannah[6], Olive[6], Lucy[6], Polly[6], Simeon[6], Anis[6], George B.[6] and James[6].

d. Elsie Walker

born circa 1777 in Columbia County, New York. She died soon after June 5, 1865 at Middlefield, Otsego County, New York. She married Robert

J.[6] Bullis circa 1795, probably in Columbia County, New York. He was born circa 1771 in Columbia County, New York. He died sometime before 1855 at Middlefield, Otesgo County, New York. His father was Robert J.[5] [Thomas[4] {of Greenwich, Fairfield County, Connecticut}, John[3], Thomas[2] {of Boston, Suffok, Massachusetts}, Phillip[1] {of England}] Bullis of Columbia County, New York. His mother was Elizabeth [Frederick, Christian] Tobias of New York. Elsie and Robert[6] had eight children: (son)[7] [died age 11], Joseph I.[7], Avery John[7], Russell Dorr[7], Archibald[7], John[7], Catherine[7] and Andrew[7].

e. Jane Walker
born on June 15, 1788 in Columbia County, New York. She died on August 27, 1820 at Chatham, Columbia County, New York. She married Barton[6] Huested [afa Husted] on November 19, 1805 at Chatham, Columbia County, New York. He was born on April 21, 1783 at Nassau, Rensselaer County, New York. He died on August 16, 1866 in Columbia County, New York. His father was Louis[5] [David[4] {of Greenwich, Fairfield County, Connecticut}, David[3], Joseph[2], Angell[1] {of Somersetshire, England}, Robert A.[1a], Lourence[2a] {of Isle of Wight, England}, John[3a] {born circa

1519—he, a chaplain}] Husted of Dutchess County, New York. His mother was Mary Sackett of Dutchess County, New York. Jane and Barton[6] had seven children: Justus[7], Lewis[7], Barton[7], Elizabeth Ann[7], John William[7], Emmons[7] and Minard[7].

Barton[6] married, second, Rebecca Walker [the half sister of Jane Walker] on January 15, 1822 in Columbia County, New York [Editor's Note: She had married, first, Philip Lake]. She was born on February 28, 1788 in Columbia County, New York. She died on April 4, 1864, probably in Columbia County, New York. Her father was Archibald Walker of Columbia County, New York. The name of her mother is not known. Barton[6] and Rebecca had two children: Rebecca Ann[7] and Hylia[7].

   f. John A. Walker
     date and place of birth is not known.

2. Levi Pitts
   born in 1750 at Colchester, New London County, Connecticut. He died, age 91 years, 2 months, on January 20, 1856 in the area of Syracuse, Onondaga County, New York and buried there in the Walnut Grove Cemetery. He married Hannah[4] Wilbur [also found as Wilbor] sometime before July 1779

[when their child Anna was born] at either Chatham or Canaan, Columbia County, New York. She was born in 1760 at Chatham, Columbia County, New York [another record says Aurelia, Cayuga County, New York]. She died on February 4, 1842 at Onondaga Hills, Onondaga County, New York and was buried there in the Walnut Grove Cemetery. Her father was Samuel[3] [Samuel[2] {of Tiverton, Newport County, Rhode Island}, William[1] {of Braintree, Essex, England}] Wilbor of Little Compton, Newport County, Rhode Island. Her mother was Hannah Wilcox of Little Compton, Newport County, Rhode Island. Levi and Hannah[4] had six children:

a. Anna Pitts
    born on July 17, 1779 at Canaan, Columbia County, New York. She died on August 13, 1874 at Hadley, Saratoga County, New York and was buried there in the Ellis-Johnson Cemetery. She married Elijah[6] Ellis circa 1795 at Queensbury, Warren County, New York. He was born on May 11, 1775 at Shaftsbury, Bennington County, Vermont. He died on April 21, 1856 at Hadley, Saratoga County, New York and was buried there in the Ellis-Johnson Cemetery. He was a saw mill owner on the Scandaga River. His father was Amasa[5] [Reuben[4] {of Medfield, Norfolk County, Mass-

achusetts}, David[3], Eleazer[2], John[1] {of London, England}, Samuel[1a]] Ellis of Sturbridge, Worcester County, Massachusetts. His mother was Content[4] [David[3] {of Coventry, Tolland County, Connecticut}, John[2] {of Suffield, Hartland County, Connecticut}, John[1] {of England and later of Windsor, Hartford, Connecticut}, "Sir" Thomas[1a] {a Medical Doctor of Newberry Park, Windsor, England}]] Millington of Shaftsbury, Bennington County, Vermont. Anna and Elijah[6] had thirteen children: Elizabeth[7], Andrew[7], Jemmina[7], Lefa[7], (child)[7], Amy[7], Anna[7], Sybel[7], Elijah[7], Joseph H.[7], David[7], Sarah Ella[7] and Zina[7].

b. James Pitts
date and place of birth, either in Columbia or Onandaga County, New York, is not known. He died on June 28, 1867 at Onondaga Hill, Onondaga County, New York and was buried there in the Walnut Grove Cemetery.

c. Levi, Pitts, Jr.
date and place of birth, either in Columbia or Onandaga County, New York, is not known. He died on March 1, 1836 at Onandaga Hills, Onondaga County, New York and was buried there in the Walnut Grove Cemetery.

d. Truman H. Pitts
date and place of birth, either in Columbia or Onandaga County, New York, is not known. He died on March 29, 1816 at Onandaga Hills, Onandaga County, New York and was buried there in the Walnut Grove Cemetery.

e. Ulepsia [afa Ulessia] Pitts
date and place of birth, either in Columbia or Onandaga County, New York, is not known. She died on June 1, 1819 at Onandaga Hills, Onandaga County, New York and was buried there in the Walnut Grove Cemetery.

f. Betsey Pitts
born on October 19, 1799 in Onondaga County, New York. She died on December 31, 1869 in Fairfield County, Michigan. She married Edward Hodge on September 13, 1824, presumably in Onondaga County, New York. He was born on September 18, 1790 in Grafton County, New Hampshire. He died on February 13, 1862, presumably in Fairfield County, Michigan. His father was Thomas Hodge of New Hampshire. His mother was Lucy Webber of New Hampshire. Betsey and Edward had three children: Nancy J., Adelphia Kezia and Lucy E.

3. **Joseph Pitts**

   born on September 2, 1752 [another record says February 9, 1751/1752] at Chatham, Columbia County, New York. He died, age 81, of cholera on February 12, 1833 at Chatham, Columbia County, New York and was buried there in the Pitts Family Burying Ground north of Old Chatham. He married Elizabeth[5] Winans circa 1773 in New York. Elizabeth[5] was born on May 10, 1755 in Greene County, New York. She died, age 82 years, 9 months, on February 10, 1838 at Chatham, Columbia County, New York. Her father was William[4] [Conrad[3] {of Elizabethtown, Essex County, New Jersey}, Jan[2] {Winans/Eynantz}, Jan[1] {of Antwerp, Belgium}] Winans of Greene County, New York. Her mother was Sarah Hawley of Rahway, Union County, New Jersey. Joseph and Elizabeth[5] had ten children: William, James B., Lewis, Elizabeth "Betsey," Joseph, Jr., Levi, Clarinda, Waity, John W., Electra.

4. **Amasa Pitts**

   born circa 1755/1756 at Chatham, Columbia County, New York [his will, made on September 22, 1835, says he was age 79]. He died on November 19, 1839 at Chatham, Columbia County, New York. His will was recorded there on January 30, 1840. He married Mary Rosanna[4] Roberts circa 1776 at Kings District, Albany County, New York [another record says married circa 1784, but this is clearly incorrect]. She was born circa 1755 in New York. She died sometime before 1836 at Chatham, Columbia County, New York. Her father was Philip[3] [Peter[2], Peter[1] {of England}] Roberts of Providence, Providence County, Rhode Island. Her mother was Sarah Corey of Tiverton, Providence County, Rhode Island. Amasa and Mary[4] had four children:

a. Philip Pitts
   born circa 1774/1780 at Chatham, Columbia County, New York. He died on May 18, 1870 at Cooper's Plains, Steuben County, New York. He married Silence "Marie" (Unknown). Philip and Silence had four children: John M., Sally, Asahel and Samantha.

b. Sarah "Sally" Pitts
   born circa 1783 at Chatham, Columbia County, New York. She died in 1818 at Chatham, Columbia County, New York and was buried there in the Chatham Union Cemetery. She married Henry[2] Fosmire circa 1800/1810 in Columbia County, New York. He was born circa 1779 in Columbia County, New York. He died sometime prior to 1835 in Columbia County, New York. His father is Hendrick[1] Fosmer [afa Vosmer] of The Netherlands. His

mother was Catherine[2] [Johann Jonas[1] {of Rhineland-Palatinate, Neuwied, Rheinland-Pfalz, Germany}, Gerhardt[1a]] Bakers [afa Backes] of New York City, New York. Sarah and Henry[2] had four children: Betsey[3], Sally Ann[3], Catherine[3] and Garret Henry[3].

c. William Levi Pitts

born sometime before 1790 at Chatham, Columbia County, New York. His date and place of death is not known. He married Rebecca E.[6] Sheldon on December 30, 1819 in New York. She was born circa 1799 in Rhode Island. Her date and place of death is not known. Her father was John Taylor[5] [Jonathan[4], Timothy[3], Timothy[2], John[1] {of England}] Sheldon of Newport County, Rhode Island. Her mother was Hannah Rider of Dartmouth, Bristol County, Massachusetts. William Levi and Rebecca had a child: Asahel.

d. Samantha Marie Pitts

born circa 1810 [LDS records say circa 1797] at Chatham, Columbia County, New York. She died sometime between 1860 and 1870 at Orange, Steuben County, New York [she last appeared on the 1860 U. S. Census; her husband Abraham had remarried by the 1870 U. S. Census]. She married Abraham H. Scott on

December 14, 1830. He was born circa 1805/1806 at Cobelskill, Schoharie County, New York. He died on February 27, 1886 at Campbell, Steuben County, New York. Living with him on the 1850 U. S. Census was his son Adelbert, his wife and an unnamed child]. His father was Jacob H. Scott of Cobleskill, Schoharie County, New York. His mother was Magda[1] "Lena" (Unknown) of Germany. Samantha and Abraham had seven children: Judson P., Abraham H. "Abram," Samantha Marie, Sarah Antorelia, Emily, Orelia and Adelbert A.

Abraham married, second, Moriah (Unknown) sometime before 1870 [when she first appears on the U. S. Census as his wife, living at Campbell, Steuben County, New York]. She was born circa 1810 in New York. She died sometime before 1880 [when she no longer appears on the U. S. Census with Abraham] at Campbell, Steuben County, New York.

5. William Pitts
born on December 4, 1760 at Chatham, Columbia County, New York. He died on December 27, 1839 at Nassau, Rensselaer County, New York [Editor's Note: Many researchers have confused this William Pitts with William, son of Joseph Pitts and

Elizabeth Winans].

ADDENDA PAGE

Pg Ref #   Comment/Correction/Addition/Etc.

_____

_____

_____

_____

_____

_____

_____

_____

_____

_____

_____

_____

_____

_____

_____

_____

www.ingramcontent.com/pod-product-compliance
Lightning Source LLC
Chambersburg PA
CBHW020527290526
45786CB00002B/786